WHICH HAS MORE CHOLESTEROL?

4 Raw shrimp	OR	Peanut butter
Potato chips	OR	1 Cup of eggnog
1 Cup of ice cream	OR	1 Italian sausage
1 Slice of French toast	OR	1 Blueberry muffin

The cholesterol values of these and hundreds of other foods you eat all the time will surprise you. The more you know, the healthier you'll stay.

Answers:
Shrimp: 130; Peanut butter 0
Potato chips 0; Eggnog 149
Ice cream 153; Sausage 69
French toast 112; Muffin 45

THE COMPLETE CHOLESTEROL COUNTER

Penny Mintz

BALLANTINE BOOKS • NEW YORK

Copyright © 1989 by The Jeffrey Weiss Group, Inc.

All rights reserved under International and Pan-American Copyright Conventions. Published in the United States of America by Ballantine Books, a division of Random House, Inc., New York, and simultaneously in Canada by Random House of Canada Limited, Toronto.

Produced by The Jeffrey Weiss Group, Inc., 96 Morton Street, New York, New York 10014

Library of Congress Catalog Card Number: 89-91889

ISBN 0-345-36321-3

Manufactured in the United States of America

First Edition: February 1990
Third Printing: December 1991

CONTENTS ──────────────────────

Introduction. 1
Cholesterol: The #1 Risk Factor for Heart Disease
   and Stroke. 3
Diet: The First Defense Against High Cholesterol. 12
Taking Control of Your Cholesterol Intake. 18
The Two "Step Diets". 28
When All Else Fails: A Look at Cholesterol Drugs. . . . 46
Glossary. 52
Equivalent Measures. 56
Abbreviations. 57
Generic Foods. 58
Packaged Foods. 136
Restaurant Foods. 225

Introduction

In 1976 the American Legion held a convention in Philadelphia, during which twenty-nine members became mysteriously ill and died. A minor panic spread through the country about what came to be called "Legionnaire's Disease."

In recent years a much more terrifying disease has come to the fore: Acquired Immune Deficiency Syndrome. AIDS has killed over 49,000 people since 1981, more than 10,000 in 1988 alone.* Fear of AIDS has changed the way people live.

Arteriosclerosis has been a familiar disease for hundreds of years. It must be true, then, what people say: familiarity breeds contempt. How else can one explain the lack of panic over the heart attacks and strokes that result from arteriosclerosis? Over 900,000 people died from heart disease and stroke in 1987. Millions of others survived to live partially or severely restricted lives. Nearly a third of those stricken were middle-aged or younger. The irony is that many of these people could have prevented their illness or death, because, to a certain extent, heart disease and stroke are the result of the American style of life.

This book will explain just what that means in detail,

and in particular how to keep *cholesterol*—the number-one risk factor for heart disease and stroke—under control.

First you'll find out what cholesterol is: why every tissue in the body manufactures it, how "good" cholesterol differs from "bad" cholesterol, and more. Then you'll learn how to monitor your diet and create pleasing alternatives to the high-cholesterol foods you might be used to. Finally, the listings that make up the bulk of this book give you cholesterol counts and the amount of calories and fat in virtually every food you are likely to eat. Divided into several sections—generic foods (those without brand names), packaged foods, and restaurant foods—it is these numbers that will help you put your anticholesterol program into action. A good cholesterol count, and good health in general, can both be yours; you have to want them, and you have to start *today*!

The numbers for cholesterol, calorie, and fat listed in this book are given in commonly sized portions and were obtained from the United States Department of Agriculture, the individual food producers and manufacturers, and food labels.

Please note that since food makers change their ingredients, some of the values listed in this book may vary from what you find in the market. In addition, cholesterol information is not always available; many food producers and restaurant chains are still in the process of obtaining cholesterol counts for their foods, and the U.S. government does not yet require cholesterol information to appear on food packaging.

*According to the Gay Men's Health Crisis and the U.S. Department of Health and Human Services' Centers for Disease Control.

Cholesterol:
The #1 Risk Factor For Heart
Disease and Stroke _____

As a nation, we Americans eat too much fat. We consume too much salt. Our diets are too low in fiber. We get too little exercise. We're overweight. And we smoke. We may be living the "good life," but it's killing us. We are literally clogging up our arteries, the all-important canals through which our life-blood flows.

Arteries are supposed to be supple and hollow. All too often, though, they aren't. In 1710 a physiologist named William Cowper came across an artery that he described as looking like the stem of a well-used tobacco pipe, with "sides . . . so thick, and its bore consequently much lessened." In the late 1700s, Edward Jenner, who developed the smallpox vaccine, was performing an autopsy when he came upon an artery so rock-hard it put a nick in his scalpel. These scientists were seeing the effects of *arteriosclerosis*. (*Sclerosis* is a derivative of the Greek word for hardening or hardness.)

Atherosclerosis is the most common form of arteriosclerosis. It begins—often in childhood—when fatty streaks are deposited within the wall of an artery. Over the years, these fatty streaks fill up with cholesterol and other materials and turn into *plaque*. As the amount of plaque increases, the space inside the artery through which the blood can flow is reduced.

The plaque buildup on the inside wall of the artery can be likened to a lesion. But whereas most other lesions heal, these usually get bigger and uglier. Over the years, as the plaque thickens and distends, there are rarely any outward symptoms of distress—at least not until a coronary artery (one that leads to the heart) is about 70 percent blocked. At that point, there may be some chest pain, or angina pectoris. Meanwhile the plaque continues to grow, setting the stage for catastrophe.

That catastrophe can take many forms. In one scenario, a weak spot in an artery near a buildup of plaque balloons and bursts from the pressure, causing internal bleeding or a cerebrovascular accident (stroke). In another, a small clot of blood, floating through the system, catches on to the plaque, completely stopping the flow of blood to a vital organ. If the heart is affected, the result is a myocardial infarction (heart attack). If the brain is deprived, it is classified as a stroke. Whatever the case, these are serious, life-threatening events that should not be allowed to happen.

WHO ARE THE PEOPLE AT RISK?

There's no way to tell by looking at a person that arterial plaques are growing inside. But it's easy to predict who is a likely candidate. According to the American Heart Association, the following people are at risk: diabetics, smokers, and those who have high blood pressure, are overweight, or get little exercise. Any combination of these "risk factors" makes things even worse. What's the single most important risk factor? High serum cholesterol (cholesterol in the blood).

CHOLESTEROL

Cholesterol is a white, waxy substance that helps determine the properties of cell membranes; helps guarantee the smooth, uninterrupted flow of nerve impulses through the body; and is used to produce vitamin D, the sex hormones progesterone and testosterone, and the bile acids used in the digestion of fat, among other things. It is so important to the normal, smooth functioning of the human body that every tissue in the body produces it. Without it, we would die.

Cholesterol may be vital, but that hardly means we have to shovel it into our bodies. Rather, the body appears to have arranged to get all the cholesterol it needs by itself. In addition to the small amounts produced throughout the body, the liver synthesizes between 3,000 and 4,000 milligrams every day. When we eat large amounts of cholesterol, the liver produces less. When we eat smaller amounts, the liver makes up the difference. In other words, whatever cholesterol we get from our diets—dietary cholesterol is the only other source of cholesterol besides the liver—represents, for the most part, a *surplus*.

That's discouraging news for anyone looking for a simple relationship between cholesterol in the diet and serum cholesterol. Still, almost all major health organizations say that limiting cholesterol intake is one of the first steps to take if you have a cholesterol problem. And even if you don't have a cholesterol problem, keeping a lid on your intake of cholesterol is valuable because (a) you don't want to *get* a cholesterol problem, and (b) foods that are high in cholesterol are very likely high in unhealthy saturated fats as well. (Saturated fats are discussed in more detail on page 14.)

IS YOUR CHOLESTEROL TOO HIGH?

The only way to find out if your cholesterol is too high is by getting a blood test. Indeed, the National Heart, Lung, and Blood Institute (NHLBI) recommends that every person twenty years of age or older should have his or her blood tested for serum cholesterol. Portable testing machines commonly used throughout the country can generate total cholesterol counts in a matter of minutes; more detailed tests take longer.

The following chart shows the most recent federal

guidelines for cholesterol, as issued in late 1987 by the NHLBI and endorsed by the American Heart Association, the American Medical Association, and many other professional health organizations.

Total Cholesterol Levels
(milligrams of cholesterol
per deciliter of blood)

Below 200	Desirable
Between 200 and 239	Borderline
240 and above	High

If your cholesterol level is less than 200 mg/dl, your doctor will probably say, "Congratulations. You're fine. Come back in five years." (There are, however, physicians and other medical professionals who recommend even lower cholesterol levels.)

If your cholesterol level is 200 or more, you must modify your diet (how to do so is discussed in more detail on page 12). Further, you should take another blood test if you have already had heart trouble or have any *two* of the following risk factors:

- maleness (all males automatically start out with one risk factor)
- family history of premature coronary heart disease
- cigarette smoking
- high blood pressure
- diabetes
- body weight more than 20 percent above normal

The results from this second blood test include a breakdown of the cholesterol count into *low-density lipoproteins* and *high-density lipoproteins*, two measures that offer physicians a more complete cholesterol profile. Before having this second blood test, you must go without food for at least four hours.

If your cholesterol level is 240 mg/dl or higher, you are in a group whose risk of heart disease is unacceptably high.

You, too, should take a second blood test and follow your doctor's instructions for reducing your cholesterol. Research has demonstrated that the chance of dying of heart disease increases dramatically as the level of cholesterol in the blood rises. One study of a group of men aged 35–57 revealed that there were four times as many heart attack deaths among those whose cholesterol was 300 mg/dl than among those whose cholesterol was 200 mg/dl. The study also showed that *any* lowering of cholesterol level made a difference: For every 1 percent drop in cholesterol level, there was a drop of between 1.5 and 2 percent in coronary deaths.

WHAT ARE LIPOPROTEINS?

Cholesterol is an alcohol, not a fat. It is included with fat in a grouping called *lipid* because, like fat, cholesterol is insoluble in water. This means that it is also insoluble in blood. All lipids have to be chemically altered in order to be carried in the bloodstream. For cholesterol to become soluble in blood it combines with certain proteins to form lipoproteins. It is as a lipoprotein that cholesterol can be moved around the body.

LOW-DENSITY LIPOPROTEIN (LDL)

Most of the cholesterol in the bloodstream is combined in low-density lipoprotein molecules. LDLs play an important role as the transportation mode for getting cholesterol to cells throughout the body. Cells have LDL receptors on their surfaces that "grab" LDL molecules as needed as they pass along in the blood. Once caught, the LDL happily gives up its cholesterol.

However, problems arise when there is more low-density lipoprotein than there is need for cholesterol in the cells. In such cases—more frequent than not—LDLs drop off their "cargo" in places where it's not so welcome— such as arterial walls. Recent studies have shown that when cholesterol "clusters" or otherwise hangs around in an arterial wall, it combines with oxygen; in other words, it rots.

This rancid cholesterol attracts cells from the immune system, which absorb the cholesterol and get stuck in the arterial walls. These cholesterol-filled cells eventually grow into the fatty streaks that end up bulging into plaques. It is this sequence of events that has led to the labeling of LDLs as "bad" cholesterol.

Generally speaking, you want as little LDL cholesterol in your blood as possible. The following chart shows current, federally recommended low-density lipoprotein levels:

LDL Cholesterol Levels
(milligrams of LDL cholesterol
per deciliter of blood)

Below 130	Desirable
Between 130 and 159	Borderline high risk
160 and above	High risk

As a nation, we Americans have too much LDL in our bodies. A survey by the National Center for Health Statistics revealed that of 2,283 people tested between the years 1976 and 1980, over half had LDL levels that were borderline risk or worse.

VERY-LOW-DENSITY LIPOPROTEIN (VLDL)

When the liver synthesizes its 3,000 to 4,000 milligrams of cholesterol each day, most of that cholesterol becomes part of a *very-low-density lipoprotein*. The density of these large molecules is extremely low because they have more fat in them than anything else; fat is bulky but light. Once the VLDL is in the blood, this fat is removed and absorbed by various tissues. What remains is an intermediate-density lipoprotein, which is taken up by the liver and turned into a low-density lipoprotein. Thus, VLDLs are the precursors of LDLs.

HIGH-DENSITY LIPOPROTEIN (HDL)

High-density lipoproteins are high in density because they are made up mostly of protein. When they start out in the liver, they have relatively little lipid in them, but they have the ability to soak it up. Like LDLs, they move around the body. But instead of discharging cholesterol, HDLs pick up excess cholesterol from cells and cart it back to the liver. There, the cholesterol is containerized in the form of bile acid for shipment to the intestine and subsequent elimination. This is why HDLs have come to be known as "good" cholesterol. Put another way, HDLs are like the sanitation workers of the cholesterol world. A high level of HDL protects against heart disease by pulling cholesterol out of the arteries. The more HDL there is, the better.

Normal HDL levels are 45 to 50 for men and 50 to 60 for women. According to the NHLBI, an HDL level below 35 is another risk factor for developing coronary heart disease. One study showed that a person can still be at risk— *even with a total cholesterol count within the desired range*—if the HDL level is too low.

HDL levels are also used to generate two other common measures of cholesterol—the ratio of total cholesterol to HDL, and the ratio of LDL cholesterol to HDL cholesterol. For example, a total cholesterol count of 200 and an HDL level of 50 produces a ratio of 4. Dr. William Castelli, medical director of the Framingham Heart Study—a project that has for the past four decades tracked the cardiac history of residents of Framingham, Massachusetts—believes that the total cholesterol/HDL cholesterol ratio is the best indicator of coronary risk, and says that a ratio of 4.5 or higher qualifies as a risk. To put this in some perspective, here are some average ratios of certain population groups:

- vegetarians: 2.5
- marathon runners: 3.4

- female heart disease victims: 4.6–6.4
- male heart disease victims: 5.4–6.1.

CONQUERING ATHEROSCLEROSIS

Atherosclerosis has bred complacency. Sure, we say to ourselves, it's a danger, but we have time... we have time. The truth is that atherosclerosis is a lifelong problem that demands lifelong solutions. It's a terrible mistake to wait until an emergency shocks you into awareness of the problem; a coronary bypass operation is a very serious, high-tech medical procedure, and it's certainly no way to learn about the dangers of cholesterol. Once a person reaches that point, it's too late to live an essentially doctor-free life ever again.

Fortunately, most people have the power to overcome this disease. It does require making some changes in the way we live—and making them now.

A sample cholesterol report

HOSPITAL ST. SOMEWHERE ELSE
Department of Pathology and Laboratory Medicine

Lipid Profile and Interpretation

Patient: John Doe   P.I. Number: 843880
Sex: male   Physician: Dr. Dipil
Age: 61   Date of Specimen: 5/9/89

──────────── Lipid Data ────────────

TOTAL CHOLESTEROL   256 mg/dl
TOTAL TRIGLYCERIDES   143 mg/dl
LDL CHOLESTEROL   189.4 mg/dl
HDL CHOLESTEROL   38 mg/dl
VLDL CHOLESTEROL   28.6 mg/dl

──────── Risk Estimates for Coronary Artery Disease ────────
Risk based on cholesterol alone:
     HIGH risk for C.A.D.   100——200——300——400

Risk based on total chol/HDL ratio: HIGH
Risk based on LDL chol/HDL ratio: HIGH

──────────── Lipid Interpretation ────────────

SUGGESTIVE OF TYPE II A HYPERLIPIDEMIA

This patient has a "high" total level of cholesterol as defined by the National Cholesterol Education Program.

It is recommended by the committee that these patients have a second total cholesterol determination and the average of the two levels be used in the evaluation of the patient. These patients should also have lipoprotein analysis (i.e., this current study). The LDL cholesterol and HDL cholesterol levels can assist in the determination of type of treatment offered to these patients.

In addition, other risk factors for C.A.D. should be evaluated (i.e., male sex, hypertension, cigarette smoking, diabetes mellitus, severe obesity, or a history of coronary heart disease either in the patient or family members).

Diet:
The First Defense Against High Cholesterol _____

Diet is the most important defense against high cholesterol. If your cholesterol level is too high, it's likely that many of your eating habits are incompatible with the goal of keeping your dietary cholesterol at an acceptable level. That must change.

Before you make any changes in your diet, make certain that your doctor or dietician is aware of those changes and approves. Different people have different needs. Although the diet described here is the one recommended by the United States Surgeon General, based on a report issued by the National Cholesterol Education Program, the food on this diet may not meet your particular health needs. See your doctor first!

As a first step in an effort to lower blood cholesterol, the Surgeon General recommends the following:

- Fat should amount to no more than 30 percent of each day's calories. (According to *The Surgeon General's Report on Nutrition and Health* for 1988, the average American diet is 37 percent fat.)

- Saturated fat should be less than 10 percent of each day's calories.
- No more than 300 milligrams of cholesterol should be eaten per day.

You'll notice that these recommendations pay a good deal of attention to fat. Unfortunately, you cannot eliminate all fat from your diet, for it is an essential nutrient. In addition to its role in the creation of cholesterol, fat is needed to move fat-soluble vitamins through the bloodstream. What's more, people on extremely low-fat diets become more susceptible to infection, and their skin becomes red, scaly, and inflamed. Children in particular need fat for growth. *Do not put children on a fat-restricted diet unless you do so under a doctor's or nutritionist's careful supervision.*

Still, an overall decrease in fat intake has been found to lower serum cholesterol levels. If you could limit the calories you get from fat to 13 percent of your total daily intake, as the Japanese do, you would probably achieve their rate of heart disease: Japanese are one-tenth as likely as Americans to suffer from coronary heart disease. That impressive rate cannot be explained by genetic differences alone. Japanese who have moved to the United States and switched to an American diet show increased incidence of cardiovascular trouble soon after.

Fortunately, there is no need to push your fat intake all the way down to 13 percent. You may be able to lower your serum cholesterol by an acceptable amount by staying away from the kind of fat that has almost no place in the traditional Japanese diet: saturated fat.

CHOOSE UNSATURATES OVER SATURATES

The fats in foods are combinations of saturated and unsaturated fatty acids. The level to which they are saturated or unsaturated generally depends upon whether the food is of animal or vegetable origin (as we'll see, there are exceptions to this rule).

Saturated Fats

Saturated fats are of particular concern because they increase production of cholesterol in the liver and raise blood cholesterol levels even more than does dietary cholesterol. In addition, most foods containing high amounts of saturated fat are also high in cholesterol. Thus, a diet high in saturated fats puts most people at risk for developing atherosclerosis.

Animal foods such as butter, cheese, egg yolks, whole milk, and red meats—beef, pork, and lamb—contain excessive amounts of saturated fats. Foods you see advertised as "made with 100% pure vegetable shortening and cholesterol-free" are sometimes made with coconut oil and palm oil, two extremely saturated fats. Avoid these as best you can.

Monounsaturated Fats

When monounsaturated fats make up a significant part of dietary fat, the liver produces less VLDL, and it does so *without* lowering the amount of HDL. That leaves the same number of cholesterol scavengers in the bloodstream with less cholesterol to cart away—making for easier going on the body.

Olive oil and the fats found in nuts and many kinds of fish are high in monounsaturated fatty acids. The effect of monounsaturated fats may explain the low rate of heart disease in Mediterranean countries such as Greece and Italy, where olive oil is an important ingredient in the cooking. It may also explain why heart attacks are almost unknown among Eskimos, whose diet, though very high in animal fat from seals and whales, seems not to cause problems because seal oil and whale blubber are both highly monounsaturated fats. Try to include monounsaturated fats in your diet instead of saturated fats.

Polyunsaturated Fats

Like monounsaturated fats, polyunsaturated fats have been found to reduce the level of low-density lipoprotein levels in most people. Unfortunately, polyunsaturates also lower the level of protective HDL and appear to have a variety of other negative effects. One experiment showed that a high-polyunsaturate, low-cholesterol diet damages a person's ability to metabolize cholesterol. Polyunsaturated fats have also been associated with the formation of gallstones and free radicals (unstable, highly reactive chemical compounds that attack healthy cells), and can cause red blood cells to clump together in the capillaries—the narrowest corridors of the bloodstream—impeding the flow of oxygen and other nutrients.

The American Heart Association recommends limited consumption of polyunsaturated fats, which are found in safflower oil, sunflower oil, corn oil, soybean oil, cottonseed oil, and sesame oil.

YOUR IDEAL WEIGHT

Overweight people have higher LDLs, lower HDLs, higher blood pressure, and an increased incidence of diabetes mellitus. People whose weight is considered ideal for their height and weight are rewarded with a lower level of LDL, a higher level of HDL, and, most likely, a sleek, handsome body to boot. Consult the following charts for your ideal weight and then strive to reach it!

SAY YES TO FIBER

Because of the grave dangers presented by high cholesterol levels, thousands of studies have been done in the hopes of discovering additional cholesterol-lowering strategies. So far, one of the most effective has been found to be *increasing your intake of soluble fiber*.

EAT MORE FIBER

Soluble bran fibers such as oat and rice bran lower LDL without lowering HDL. They can be found in beans, peas, oats, corn, barley, and most vegetables and fruits. Large amounts—about two-thirds of a cup a day—are needed to get good results.

Soluble brans work by increasing the amount of bile

IDEAL WEIGHT IN POUNDS FOR WOMEN

| Height | Body Frame | | |
	Small	Medium	Large
4'10"	96–104	101–113	109–120
4'11"	99–107	104–116	112–124
5'0"	102–110	107–119	115–128
5'1"	105–113	110–122	118–132
5'2"	108–116	113–126	121–134
5'3"	111–119	116–130	125–138
5'4"	114–123	120–135	129–142
5'5"	117–127	124–139	130–146
5'6"	121–131	128–143	137–148
5'7"	126–135	132–146	141–150
5'8"	130–140	136–151	145–152
5'9"	134–144	140–155	149–154
5'10"	138–148	144–159	153–158
5'11"	142–152	145–163	157–162

[Add 4 pounds for every inch above 5'11"]

acid eliminated through the large intestine. Bile acid is used during digestion to break fats into smaller molecules so that they can be absorbed through the wall of the small intestine. After serving this function, the bile, originally made by the liver from cholesterol, passes on to the large intestine. Most of it is then taken up and returned to the liver. Soluble bran fiber combines with bile, making it too big to be reabsorbed. Instead it is eliminated, forcing the liver to turn more cholesterol into new bile. With so much cholesterol production going into the creation of bile, less of it becomes VLDL. The result is a drop in serum LDL.

AND FURTHERMORE...

It's ludicrous to expect good health without being willing to stop smoking and get exercise. Smoking lowers

IDEAL WEIGHT IN POUNDS FOR MEN

Height	Body Frame		
	Small	Medium	Large
5'1"	112–120	118–129	126–141
5'2"	115–123	121–133	129–144
5'3"	118–126	124–136	132–148
5'4"	121–129	127–139	135–152
5'5"	124–133	130–143	138–156
5'6"	127–137	134–147	142–161
5'7"	132–141	138–152	147–166
5'8"	136–145	142–156	151–170
5'9"	140–150	146–160	155–174
5'10"	144–154	150–165	159–179
5'11"	148–158	154–169	163–183
6'	152–162	158–175	168–189
6'1"	156–167	162–180	173–194
6'2"	160–171	167–185	178–199
6'3"	164–175	172–190	182–204

[Add four pounds for every inch above 6'3"]

HDL and is an independent risk factor for coronary heart disease. Exercise helps *raise* HDL. Studies have shown that people who exercise regularly have higher HDL levels than sedentary people. Try to get a thirty-minute aerobic workout at least three times a week. You'll feel calmer, look younger, and have more energy.

A PLAN OF ATTACK

The next section of this book provides nuts-and-bolts guidelines for eating less fat, choosing monounsaturates over other types of fat, and staying lean by keeping track of calories, fat, and cholesterol. Lowering cholesterol is a big job, just like restoring a house. But once the trauma of moving day is past and you begin adjusting to your new neighborhood, you'll find it will be worth the work.

Takinq Control of Your Cholesterol Intake _____

If your serum cholesterol is high, *The Complete Cholesterol Counter* may be a lifesaver. All the information you need to follow the U.S. Surgeon General's two "step diets" is right here.

The "step-one" diet involves lowering fat intake to 30 percent of each day's calories, limiting saturated fat to one-third of total fat, and eating less than 300 milligrams of cholesterol per day. You don't have to be a rocket scientist to do the calculations required to follow these diets, but you do have to be able to count calories. You also have to keep track of cholesterol content. And you have to know a bit more about fats.

CALCULATING CALORIES

To keep fat intake below 30 percent, you need to know what your optimum daily caloric intake should be.

First, look up your ideal weight in the tables on pages 16 and 17. *Note: Since your ideal weight is where you must be, you should use that weight, even if it has been a while since you've seen it on your bathroom scale.*

Next, multiply your ideal weight by 13 to get the

number of calories you should eat each day. Why 13? Because it takes about 13 calories per pound to maintain your weight. If you are extremely active, it may take more than 13 calories per pound to maintain your weight; in this case, add another one or two calories per pound. If you are inactive, subtract a calorie or two per pound (and take a walk —a long, brisk walk—every day).

The following example shows these two simple steps put into action for a woman with an ideal weight of 135 pounds.

$$\text{Ideal weight} \times 13 \text{ calories per day} = \text{Optimum calories per day}$$
$$135 \times 13 = 1755 \text{ cal/day}$$

If you have a great deal of weight to lose, 13 times your ideal weight might be too few calories. In that case, pick an intermediate weight goal, and multiply that number by 13. Then, when you reach that weight, go down to the next level. Continue in this way as required. Weight loss should be done *slowly*—and should be accompanied by regular exercise. When you lose weight quickly, you lose muscle rather than fat. That leaves you with more fat relative to muscle, the opposite of what you want.

Once you have found your desired daily calorie intake, write it at the bottom of a Daily Food Chart (see the sample on page 00). There is a space for your total calorie goal just beneath the line where you record the amount you actually consume.

FIGURING FOR FAT

Your daily intake of calories from fat must be less than 30 percent of the day's total. Thus, our 135-pound woman, maintaining her weight with 1755 calories per day, would keep her fat intake below 526 calories a day.

$$\text{Calories per day} \times 30 \text{ percent} = \text{Calories of fat per day}$$
$$1755 \times .30 = 526 \text{ cal/day}$$

Daily Food Chart			
Food Eaten	Total Cal.	Fat Cal.	Chol. (mg)
Breakfast			
Lunch			
Dinner			
Snacks			

	Total Cal.	Fat Cal.	Chol. (mg)
Totals	———	———	———
Goals	———	———	———

To figure out your daily fat goal, multiply your caloric goal by 30 percent. Put that figure in the space provided at the bottom of your Daily Food Chart.

On the last of the goal lines, write the amount of cholesterol you are permitted. That number is 300 milligrams for the step-one diet and 200 milligrams for the step-two diet.

As the day goes by, write everything you eat in the Food column. Then go to the appropriate section of this book's *listings* for the rest of the data. Total calories, fat calories, and milligrams of cholesterol are provided for generic foods, a wide range of packaged foods, and the menus of many restaurant chains.

To find out how much of the fat is saturated fat, use the following chart, which shows the percentages of saturated, monounsaturated, and polyunsaturated fats in a large number of foods. You'll note that the percentages do not add up to 100; the balance is made up of protein, carbohydrates, fiber, minerals, and the other elements that make up any food.

Multiply the total calories of a food by its percentage of saturated fat to get its saturated-fat content. If the exact food is missing, substitute something similar. This chart can be used to determine which foods to eat as well as which to avoid. Remember, monounsaturates are best for you.

FATTY ACID PERCENTAGES

Food	% Sat	% Mono	% Poly
Dairy Products			
Cream, heavy	23	11	1
Cream, light	19	9	.7
Cheese			
Cheddar	21	10	1
Cottage, creamed	3	1	.1
Cream	22	10	1
Swiss	18	8	1
Milk, whole	2	1	tr
Sour cream	13	6	.7
Yogurt, low-fat	1	.4	tr
Eggs	3	4	1
Fats and Oils			
Butter	66	30	4
Beef fat	52	44	4
Chicken fat	31	47	22

Food	%Sat	%Mono	%Poly
Coconut oil	87	11	2
Corn oil	13	25	62
Cottonseed oil	25	25	50
Lard	41	48	11
Margarine	16	36	26
Mayonnaise	12	23	41
Olive oil	14	77	9
Peanut oil	18	49	33
Safflower oil	10	13	77
Soybean, hydrogenated	15	24	61
Sunflower	11	20	69
Vegetable shortening	26	46	28

Poultry (cooked)

Food	%Sat	%Mono	%Poly
Chicken	3	5	3
Chicken liver	2	2	1
Duck, lean	4	4	1
Turkey	2	1	2

Meat (cooked)

Food	%Sat	%Mono	%Poly
Bacon	17	27	6
Bologna	11	13	2
Beef, eye round, lean	3	3	.2
Beef, ground	8	9	1
Beef, sirloin, lean	4	4	.4
Frankfurter	11	14	3
Ham slices	3	5	1
Lamb, lean	4	4	.6
Pork, lean	4	5	1
Salami, dry	12	17	3
Veal, lean	7	7	1

Nuts

Food	%Sat	%Mono	%Poly
Almond, raw	5	34	11
Cashew, roasted	9	27	8
Peanut, roasted in oil	7	25	16
Pistachio nuts	6	33	8
Walnut	6	14	40

Food	%Sat	%Mono	%Poly
Seafood			
Clam, steamed	1	1	3
Cod, baked	1	1	3
Fish sticks, frozen, cooked	10	17	10
Flounder, baked	3	2	3
Herring, pickled	8	41	6
Lobster, steamed	1	1	1
Mussel, steamed	4	5	6
Oyster, raw	8	3	10
Scallop, fried	11	19	12
Salmon, smoked	7	15	8
Salmon, cooked	6	13	16
Sardine, canned in oil	7	17	22
Shrimp, steamed	3	2	4
Striped bass, raw	5	6	7
Swordfish, baked	8	11	7
Trout, baked	5	8	9
Tuna, canned in oil	7	13	13
Tuna, canned in water	1	1	1

KEEPING TRACK WHEN YOU COOK AT HOME

The listings in this book include virtually every food you eat at home. Just measure what you use, then look it up in the section called *Generic Foods* (page 58). You might have to do a bit of simple arithmetic, but for the most part the measurements provided are common-sized portions.

KEEPING TRACK OF PACKAGED FOODS

Most name-brand foods have not yet been tested for cholesterol content, but plenty have. The section called *Packaged Foods* (page 136) lists many supermarket foods alphabetically by brand.

A Word About Reading Labels

If a name-brand food is missing from the *Packaged Foods* section, it may be possible to get the information you need from the label. The federal government requires nutritional information to be printed on the package of any food that makes a health claim or includes a food additive. This information always shows the number of calories in the food and the number of grams of fat. Some labels break down fat content into grams of saturates, monounsaturates, and polyunsaturates. A few also include the number of milligrams of cholesterol in the food.

For example, Campbell's Cream of Asparagus Soup has the following information on the side of its can:

NUTRITION INFORMATION PER SERVING

SERVING SIZE.........................4 oz—CONDENSED
(8 oz AS PREPARED—226 g)

SERVINGS PER CONTAINER.............. 2 ¾
CALORIES.............................. 90
   PROTEIN (GRAMS).................... 2
   TOTAL CARBOHYDRATES (GRAMS)..... 11
      SIMPLE SUGARS (GRAMS).......... 3
      COMPLEX CARBOHYDRATES
      (GRAMS)......................... 8
   FAT (GRAMS)........................ 4
   SODIUM............................. 938 mg/serving

PERCENTAGE OF U.S. RECOMMENDED DAILY ALLOW-
ANCES (U.S. RDA)

PROTEIN	2	RIBOFLAVIN	2
VITAMIN A	4	NIACIN	*
VITAMIN C	2	CALCIUM	*
THIAMINE	*	IRON	*

*CONTAINS LESS THAN 2% OF THE U.S. RDA OF THESE NU-
TRIENTS

It's easy to get the number of total calories from this label. Each eight-ounce serving has 90. How much of that is fat? Do not be misled by the small figure (4 grams) given for fat. Each gram of fat provides 9 calories of food energy. When you take fat content from a label, multiply that number by 9 before you list it on your Daily Food Chart. Therefore, each cup of Campbell's Cream of Asparagus Soup has 36 calories of fat.

$$1 \text{ gram of fat} = 9 \text{ calories}$$
$$4 \text{ grams} \times 9 \text{ calories/gram} = 36 \text{ calories}$$

The cholesterol content of Campbell's Cream of Asparagus Soup is not on the product's label. Instead we'll have to do a little more work to find out what this figure is. Look up "cream of asparagus soup, condensed" in the *Generic Foods* section of this book. The example listed has 12 milligrams of cholesterol, but it also has more than twice the calories and fat content than our sample serving from Campbell's. This means that the serving size of our generic listing is probably over twice as large as well. Therefore, since all the cholesterol in the soup is likely to be in its fat, assume that the serving described on the label would contain about half as much cholesterol—6–7 milligrams—as that of our generic listing.

Next you'll want to know what kinds of fats are in the soup. For this information, look at the ingredients listed on the label. Nearly all packaged foods list the ingredients that went into its preparation; these are given in size order, with the largest ingredients first. Always read these lists to find out exactly which fats are included.

The label on Campbell's Cream of Asparagus Soup is as follows:

INGREDIENTS: WATER, ASPARAGUS, WHEAT FLOUR, WHEY, PARTIALLY HYDROGENATED VEGETABLE OILS (SOYBEAN OR COTTONSEED OIL), SALT, SUGAR, BUTTER, CORN STARCH, DRIED DAIRY BLEND (WHEY, CALCIUM CASEINATE), MARGARINE (PARTIALLY HYDROGENATED SOY-

BEAN OIL, WATER AND BETA CAROTENE FOR
COLOR), MONOSODIUM GLUTAMATE, YEAST EX-
TRACT AND HYDROLYZED PLANT PROTEIN, SOY
PROTEIN ISOLATE AND NATURAL FLAVORING.

The fats in Campbell's Cream of Asparagus Soup, in
size order, are partially hydrogenated soybean or cottonseed oil, butter, and partially hydrogenated soybean oil.
Hydrogenated vegetable oils are those that have been saturated with hydrogen. This turns them from liquids into
solids and thus, from the manufacturer's point of view, into
a product that is more easily stored and more pleasing to
look at. Unfortunately, the hydrogenation process also
makes these vegetable oils high in unhealthy saturated and
polyunsaturated fats, both unhealthy. Avoid packaged
foods with these ingredients, even if the label says "No
Cholesterol."

In addition, when a company lists two or more fats that
may be included, they are leaving themselves freedom to
choose the fat that is most available—and usually cheap-
est—at the time the food is actually prepared. In such
cases, always assume the worst. This is because the more
saturated fats have longer shelf lives and are generally less
costly.

Keep these tips in mind when choosing packaged foods:

- Translate fat content from grams to calories. There are 9
  calories in every gram of fat.
- Check the ingredient list for fats and oils that you can
  identify as saturated or polyunsaturated. Avoid them if
  possible.
- When a label lists several oils that may or may not be
  included, assume the worst.

KEEPING TRACK IN A RESTAURANT

The restaurant listings in this book provide calorie content, fat content in calories, and cholesterol content of the
foods in many of the country's popular chains. This book
couldn't begin to include the menus of *all* your favorite

neighborhood restaurants, but don't let that keep you from eating out. Use the section on generic foods to get an approximate idea of the content of everything you eat. And keep these tips in mind:

- Choose fish or chicken over red meat.
- Trim away all visible fat.
- Order foods that are broiled, baked, or steamed rather than sautéed or fried.
- Push all sauces aside, with the exception of tomato sauce.
- Order salad with dressing on the side. A tablespoon of dressing is more than enough (most restaurants give you way too much).
- Use yogurt with your baked potato instead of sour cream or butter.
- Stay away from pies, cakes, and pastries. If you must have dessert, order brandied fruit, angel food cake, or gelatin desserts, all of which are lower in sugar.

The general idea is to keep track of everything you eat and to avoid saturated fats. Simply by eating wisely, whether at home or out, you may be able to lower your serum cholesterol level by as much as 20 percent. For most people, that is enough to get to a relatively safe level.

The Two "Step Diets"

THE STEP-ONE DIET

M.M. is a retired, seventy-year-old woman enjoying good health. She has her cholesterol tested every year when she goes in for her general checkup. Her total serum cholesterol level is usually in the 200 to 220 range, but since she is free of any other risk factors, she had never taken any steps to lower that figure. In June 1988, just before going on vacation, Ms. M.'s cholesterol level was found to be 263. Her doctor placed her on the Step-One Diet. When M.M. went back for a second cholesterol test six months later, her total serum cholesterol had declined to 207.

The Step-One Diet is easy enough for most people to maintain. Just follow these guidelines:

- Limit yourself to eating two or three eggs a week.
- Cut back on butter. Use olive oil or margarine instead.
- Stay away from organ meats.
- Remove all visible fat from meat and chicken before you cook it.
- Poach, broil, or roast your fish, poultry, and meats instead of frying them.
- Substitute fish or poultry for meat several times a week.

- Eat sherbet, ice milk, nonfat frozen yogurt, or tofu desserts instead of ice cream.

If the Step-One Diet is a drastic change, do it in stages. And if you backslide, don't give up—just start over again.

THE STEP-TWO DIET

H.K. is a thirty-eight-year-old advertising executive. Since his uncle died of heart disease when H.K. was a child, and his father had a fatal heart attack at age fifty-seven, H.K. learned early that he was in a high-risk group. Unfortunately, H.K. has a hard time denying himself cream sauces and custard desserts when others around him are indulging. So when his serum cholesterol level reached 363 one year, Mrs. K. put him on the Step-One Diet, and then, after three months, on the Step-Two Diet. Now, despite an occasional slice of pizza or pie a la mode, H.K.'s cholesterol level is at 306 and falling.

The U.S. Surgeon General's Step-Two Diet puts further restrictions on fats and cholesterol. While calorie intake from fat should be the same as with the Step-One Diet—30 percent of total caloric intake—calories from saturated fat should be just 7 percent of total calories, and cholesterol intake should be less than 200 milligrams per day.

You should go on the Step-Two Diet if the Step-One Diet fails to bring your serum cholesterol level low enough within three-months' time. Add these tips to those you're supposed to follow for the Step-One Diet:

- Substitute two egg whites for a whole egg in any recipe.
- Use low-fat yogurt instead of sour cream on baked potatoes and in recipes.
- Stay away from butter. Substitute olive oil, vegetable oil, or margarine, and try to use half your usual amount.
- Eat less protein and make up for the lost calories with pasta, bread, and rice.
- Eat more fruit and less dessert.
- Use a microwave to cook without fats.

A low-fat diet need not be an unpalatable one. In fact, most people who go on a low-fat diet come to prefer the lighter foods and more delicate tastes. Look over the following sample menus for some tempting meal and snack ideas; recipes are included for those with asterisks. The meals offered for this sample week can be switched and rearranged to provide a month or more of variety.

SAMPLE MENUS

DAY 1	Cal	Fat Cal	Chol
Breakfast			
orange juice, ½ C	55	tr	0
*apple cinnamon bran muffins, 2	380	44	0
coffee or tea, 2 C	0	0	0
2% milk, ½ C	60	23	9
Lunch			
Arby's Regular Roast Beef	353	138	39
Arby's French Fries	215	90	8
diet soda	0	0	0
Dinner			
*lemon ginger cod, 3 oz	124	42	47
broccoli, 4 spears	200	4	0
Kraft's Red Wine Vinegar & Oil Dressing, 1 T	50	37	0
*mashed potatoes, ½ C	181	9	2
Snacks			
1 Columbo Low-fat Lite Strawberry Yogurt	190	80	5
1 mango	135	1	0
TOTAL	**1945**	**468**	**110**

DAY 2

	Cal	Fat Cal	Chol

Breakfast

	Cal	Fat Cal	Chol
Raisin Bran cereal, 1.4 oz	120	1	0
2% milk, ½ C	60	23	9
1 banana	105	9	0
coffee, 2 C	0	0	0
2% milk, ½ C	60	23	9

Lunch

	Cal	Fat Cal	Chol
turkey salad sandwich made with 1 T imitation mayonnaise on white toast	245	69	39
tomato slices	5	0	0
Rold Gold Pretzel Sticks, 2 oz	220	18	0
iced tea, instant, unsweetened	0	0	0

Dinner

	Cal	Fat Cal	Chol
*Pasta della Salute	409	246	0
baked chicken breast	140	84	73
Italian bread, 2 oz	157	5	0
*pears in liqueur	149	37	0

Snacks

	Cal	Fat Cal	Chol
grapes, ¼ lb	150	tr	0
apple, large	125	9	0
TOTAL	**1825**	**523**	**130**

DAY 3

Breakfast

	Cal	Fat Cal	Chol
cottage cheese, 1 C creamed	215	84	31
blueberries, ½ C	40	5	0
strawberries, ½ C	23	4	0
coffee, 2 C	0	0	0
2% milk, ½ C	60	23	9

	Cal	Fat Cal	Chol
Lunch			
tuna salad sandwich on rye	318	106	40
tomato slices	5	0	0
Lay's Potato Chips, 1 oz	150	93	0
orange juice, 10 oz	138	tr	0
Dinner			
*chicken with oranges and rosemary	171	61	73
baked potato with yogurt and chives	238	4	2
steamed fresh peas, ½ C	67	2	0
Snacks			
*Sweet Sherry Aspic	152	0	0
sweet cherries, 1 C	104	13	0
4 crackers with gouda cheese, 2 oz	237	145	6
TOTAL	**1918**	**540**	**161**

DAY 4

Breakfast			
prune juice, 1 C	180	0	0
vanilla yogurt, 8 oz	194	27	11
rolled oats, ¼ C	36	5	0
raisins, ¼ C	109	2	0
coffee, 2 C	0	0	0
2% milk, ½ C	60	23	9
Lunch			
chunky vegetable soup, 1 C	122	34	0
open-faced grilled Swiss cheese on rye	205	120	26
iced tea, instant, unsweetened	0	0	0

	Cal	Fat Cal	Chol
Dinner			
roast pork, lean, 3 oz	210	112	67
apple sauce, unsweetened, ½ C	53	0	0
string beans, 1 C	142	1	0
1 T grated Parmesan for string beans	25	19	4
brown rice with sauteed onion, 1 C	262	37	11
Snacks			
orange, peeled and sliced	60	0	0
*guacamole with	167	143	0
Doritos Taco Flavor Tortilla Chips, 1 oz	140	65	0
TOTAL	**1965**	**588**	**128**

DAY 5

	Cal	Fat Cal	Chol
Breakfast			
½ cantaloupe	94	7	0
*baked cottage cheese on cinnamon bread	298	39	10
coffee, 1 C	0	0	0
2% milk, ¼ C	30	12	5
Lunch			
bagel	200	19	0
*phony cream cheese	72	7	6
smoked salmon, 3 oz	99	34	20
tomato slices	5	0	0
coffee, 1 C	0	0	0
2% milk, ¼ C	30	12	5

	Cal	Fat Cal	Chol
Dinner			
*pasta primavera	697	98	19
red wine, 3½ oz	75	0	0
*Granite of Pinot Noir with fresh berries	267	3	0
Snack			
Columbo Nonfat Lite Vanilla Yogurt	160	9	5
TOTAL	**2027**	**240**	**70**

DAY 6

	Cal	Fat Cal	Chol
Breakfast			
½ grapefruit	40	0	0
hot oat bran cereal made with skim milk and ¼ cup raisins	304	21	4
coffee, 1 C	0	0	0
2% milk, ¼ C	30	12	5
Lunch			
chef salad (spinach, lettuce, cucumber, tomato, 1 slice ham and turkey, 2 T low-fat Italian dressing)	224	59	46
Italian bread, 2 oz	157	5	0
cranberry juice cocktail	147	1	0
Dinner			
*Spaghetti al Tonno e Capperi	623	459	85
½ baked beefsteak tomato	24	2	0
Snacks			
*low-fat milkshake	236	23	4
canned peaches, 1 C	44	0	0
angel food cake, 1 slice	125	0	0
TOTAL	**1954**	**582**	**144**

DAY 7	Cal	Fat Cal	Chol

Breakfast

	Cal	Fat Cal	Chol
orange juice, 1 C	110	0	0
oatmeal made with 1 C skim milk			
and ½ oz raisins	211	0	4
coffee, 1 C	0	0	0
2% milk, ¼ C	30	12	5

Lunch

	Cal	Fat Cal	Chol
Taco Bell Fajita Steak Taco with			
Guacamole	269	123	14
cola soda	160	0	0

Dinner

	Cal	Fat Cal	Chol
salmon baked with onions and			
mushrooms (sauteed in olive			
oil)	189	112	47
*beet salad with jicama, red onion			
& orange	172	87	0
rice, 1 C, with 1 pat of butter	260	35	11
white wine, 3½ oz	80	0	0

Snacks

	Cal	Fat Cal	Chol
*apple cinnamon bran muffin	190	22	0
4 graham crackers with	120	9	0
2 T peanut butter	190	149	0
TOTAL	**1871**	**549**	**81**

RECIPES

Apple Cinnamon Bran Muffins

Cal: 190
Fat Cal: 22
Chol: 0

1½ C oat bran
¾ C rice bran or polish
1½ t cinnamon
1 T baking powder
¼ C chopped walnuts
C raisins
¼ C sugar

½ C skim milk
¾ C apple cider
2 egg whites
2 T vegetable oil
1 large apple, peeled and
    diced

1. Preheat your oven to 425°.
2. Mix the dry ingredients.
3. Mix the rest of the ingredients and add them to the dry
   ingredients.
4. Pour the batter into 12 muffin cups and bake for 17
   minutes. Do not overcook. The muffins should be moist
   inside.

Makes 12 muffins

Baked Cottage Cheese

Cal: 298
Fat Cal: 39
Chol: 10

½ C low-fat (1%) cottage
    cheese
2 slices raisin bread

¼ t sugar
cinnamon

1. Spread ¼ C of cottage cheese over each piece of bread. Distribute the sugar evenly, and sprinkle on cinnamon to taste.
2. Bake at 350° about 10 minutes or until cheese begins to melt.

Serves 1

Beet Salad with Jicama, Red Onion, and Orange
   by Brendan Walsh, former chef, Arizona 206, NYC

Cal: 172
Fat Cal: 87
Chol: 0

8 medium beets
¼ C olive oil
¼ C Champagne or white wine vinegar
1 medium jicama, peeled and cut in julienne strips

3–4 navel oranges
1 small red onion, slivered
6 C baby mustard greens, washed and chilled
1 bunch chives
kosher salt and freshly ground pepper to taste

1. Cook the beets in salted water to cover until cooked through but not totally soft.
2. As the beets are cooking, whisk together oil, vinegar, and seasonings.
3. Drain and peel beets while still warm. Slice thin. Pour half the vinaigrette over the beets, and toss to cover thoroughly. Set aside.
4. Slice the stem and navel ends from the oranges. Stand orange on cut end and with a small sharp knife peel the remaining skin and pith from orange. Remove sections and place in a bowl.
5. Place 1 cup of baby mustard greens in the center of each plate. Toss jicama julienne, red onion slivers, and orange sections lightly in remaining vinaigrette, and di-

vide evenly among greens. Place sliced beets in center of each plate, and top with 3 whole chives.

Serves 6

Chicken with Oranges and Rosemary

Cal: 171
Fat Cal: 61
Chol: 73

4 chicken breasts	**1 T olive oil**
2 oranges, sliced, peels on	**salt and pepper to taste**
1 sprig fresh rosemary	

1. Preheat the oven to 350°.
2. Line a baking dish with the orange slices.
3. Brush the chicken on both sides with the olive oil.
4. Put the chicken over the oranges in the baking dish. Add rosemary leaves, salt, and pepper.
5. Bake for 1¼ hours, basting occasionally.

Serves 4

Granite of Pinot Noir with Fresh Berries
by Gerard Panguad, chef, Aurora, NYC

Cal: 267
Fat Cal: 3
Chol: 0

1 C sugar	**¼ lb strawberries**
1 C water	**¼ lb blackberries**
3 C Pinot Noir	**¼ lb raspberries**
1 orange, juice only	**6 mint leaves**
1 lemon, juice only	

1. Combine sugar and water in a pot and bring to a boil. Remove from stove to cool. When the syrup has

cooled, add both citrus juices and Pinot Noir. Mix well with a whisk.
2. Transfer the mixture to a shallow pan and freeze, stirring once an hour (gently with a fork) to break up the top frozen layer.
3. The granite is ready when it has reached a consistency similar to ice shavings. It takes at least 8 hours.
4. Spoon a small amount of the granite into each of six glasses. Add the mixed berries and cover with more granite. Garnish with a mint leaf.

Serves 6

Guacamole
by Josefina Howard, chef, Rosa Mexicano, NYC

Cal: 167
Fat Cal: 143
Chol: 0

Paste:

½ t finely minced jalapeno or serrano chili	2 t chopped coriander
2 T chopped onion	¼ t salt

Guacamole:

1 avocado (preferably Hass)	1 heaping T coriander
2 heaping T chopped onion	¼ t minced jalapeno chili
3 t chopped tomato (using just the outside part)	salt to taste

Paste:
Put all ingredients in mixing bowl. Using the back of a wooden spoon, thoroughly mash until you get a juicy paste.

Guacamole:
1. Split avocado in half lengthwise and remove the seed. Section the inside into approximately ½-inch cubes. Stir these chunks into the mixing bowl until all the avocado is thoroughly coated with the paste.
2. Add the onion, tomato, coriander, jalapeno chili, and salt. Stir. This guacamole will be mildly hot. Add more jalapeno if you desire a more spicy hotness.

Serves 2

Lemon Ginger Cod

Cal: 124
Fat Cal: 42
Chol: 47

3 oz cod	**fresh pepper**
1 pat butter	**1 t soy sauce**
½ t grated ginger	**3 lemon slices**

1. Preheat oven to 350°.
2. Wash the fish and sprinkle on ginger, pepper, and soy sauce.
3. Distribute thin slices of butter evenly over fish. Place lemon slices on top.
4. Bake 20 minutes or until the meat flakes when forked.

Serves 1

Low-fat Milkshake

Cal: 236
Fat Cal: 23
Chol: 4

1 C skim milk	**1 C strawberries**
6 ice cubes	**1 banana**

1. Put the milk and fruit in a blender and blend until smooth.
2. Add the ice cubes one at a time until crushed.

Serves 1

Mashed Potatoes

Cal: 181
Fat Cal: 9
Chol: 2

2 general purpose potatoes	**½ C skim milk**
water to cover	**¼ t chicken fat**
2 t safflower oil	**salt to taste**

1. Peel and quarter potatoes. Place them in the water and boil until soft.
2. Pour the water off and save it. Add the oil, milk, chicken fat, and salt. Mash until smooth. If more liquid is needed, add cooking water.

Serves 2

Pasta Della Salute
by Giovanna DiBernardo, owner, Cambio, NYC

Cal: 409
Fat Cal: 246
Chol: 0

10 ripe pear tomatoes	**1 lb penne**
1 bunch of fresh basil	**½ t salt**
1 clove garlic, sliced	**pepper**
½ C extra-virgin olive oil	

1. Start water for the pasta. Add salt. Add the pasta when the water reaches a boil and cook *al dente*.
2. Cut the tomatoes in half and remove the seeds. Cut 10 basil leaves in strips and set aside as garnish.

3. Little by little, put the tomato, uncut basil, garlic, and olive oil in a food processor and blend.
4. Mix sauce with cold or hot pasta. Garnish with basil strips.

Serves 4

Pasta Primavera

Cal: 697
Fat Cal: 98
Chol: 19

1 C broccoli florets (frozen is fine)
1 small zucchini, quartered and cut in 1" pieces
1 C string beans, cut in 1" pieces
1 C green peas (frozen is fine)
¼ t dried red pepper flakes
1 T olive oil
1 clove garlic, sliced
2 C mushrooms, sliced

salt and pepper to taste
4 ripe red tomatoes, skinned and cut into 1" cubes
¼ C fresh basil, chopped
1 lb Italian spaghetti
2 t butter
½ C skim milk, heated
1 T flour
⅔ C freshly grated Parmesan cheese

1. Steam separately the broccoli, zucchini, string beans, and peas. They should be crisp but tender. Mix them together and add the pepper flakes.
2. Saute the garlic in olive oil until it is brown. Then remove. Lightly saute the mushrooms in the same oil. Add salt and pepper to taste. Add the tomato and basil, and cook gently for 15 minutes.
3. Heat the milk.
4. In a pot large enough to hold the spaghetti and vegetables, melt the butter. Add the flour, stirring constantly for 3 minutes. Add the hot milk while stirring with a

wire whisk. Cook on a low flame for 20 minutes, or until it thickens.

5. Get the spaghetti cooking.
6. When the flour and milk has thickened, add the cheese. Mix until smooth.
7. Add the vegetable mixture to the tomatoes, and heat through.
8. When the spaghetti is done, drain and mix with the cheese sauce. Pour the vegetable mixture over the top and serve.

Serves 4

Pears in Liqueur

Cal: 149
Fat Cal: 37
Chol: 0

4 pears, peeled, cored, and quartered	1 T sugar
1 C orange juice	2 T liqueur

1. Mix the juice, sugar, and liqueur.
2. Marinate the pears in the mixture in the refrigerator for an hour or more.

Serves 4

Phony Cream Cheese

Cal: 72
Fat Cal: 7
Chol: 6

½ C uncreamed cottage cheese	1 T plain yogurt

Mash the ingredients together thoroughly.

Serves 1

Spaghetti al Tonno e Capperi
>   *by Giovanna DiBernardo, owner, Cambio, NYC*

Cal: 623
Fat Cal: 459
Chol: 85

1 lb spaghetti	½ C chopped parsley
½ t salt	¼ C extra-virgin olive oil
½ fresh tuna steak	¼ t fresh ground pepper
2 T capers, rinsed and drained	1 lemon, peeled and sliced thin

1. Start water for the pasta. Add salt. Add the pasta when the water reaches a boil and cook *al dente*.
2. Cut the tuna into small pieces.
3. Fry the lemon slices in the olive oil for about 5 minutes, until they begin to soften. Add the capers. Cook for a few minutes. Then add the tuna, and cook 5 more minutes.
4. Pour the contents of the pan over the drained pasta. Add the chopped parsley. Mix and serve.

Serves 4

Sweet Sherry Aspic
>   *by Josefina Howard, chef, Rosa Mexicano, NYC*

Cal: 152
Fat Cal: 0
Chol: 0

1½ T unflavored gelatin	1 egg white
½ C cold water	⅓ C sweet cream sherry
1 C sugar	1 cinnamon stick
½ lemon	2 C cold water

1. Dissolve the gelatin in the ½ cup of cold water.
2. Over medium heat combine remaining water, sugar,

cinnamon, lemon juice, and egg white, stirring constantly with wire whisk.

3. When mixture is hot, add dissolved gelatin. Continue to stir with whisk until the liquid comes to a boil.
4. Remove from heat and stir in sherry.
5. Strain through double cheese cloth. Pour into stemmed sherry glasses, and refrigerate until set.

Serves 6

When All Else Fails:
A Look at Cholesterol Drugs _____

H.W. is a fifty-eight-year-old man who trades stock options on the American Stock Exchange, a high-stress line of work if ever there was one. In 1982 he suffered a mild heart attack and underwent triple-bypass surgery. "It was really nothing," he said about this costly and common, though major, operation. "I got right up and was back at work in three weeks. I felt terrific."

Even with this impressive recovery, Mr. W. took the smart precaution of going first on the Step-One Diet and later on the Step-Two Diet. "I used basic good sense, really, eating fish, chicken, pasta, no eggs, and very little meat. I did have the occasional hamburger at summer cookouts. Besides that, I began using oat bran as a hot cereal every morning."

Despite his good sense, in December 1986 H.W.'s serum cholesterol count was 248, and his LDL was 192, both dangerously high numbers for a man with his history. So his doctor put him on a new drug called lovastatin. After nine months, his cholesterol level dropped to a comfortable 170, and his LDL declined to 108. Still, H.W. will have to be maintained on lovastatin for the rest of his life.

NO PANACEA

This case illustrates a very fundamental point about "cholesterol drugs": They are *not* an easy out, an answer for those who want a high-fat diet and low serum cholesterol. Rather, *drug therapy is the course of last resort*. It is rarely begun unless cholesterol is unacceptably high after six months of supervised dieting. The reason is simple: *All drugs have serious side effects*. Sometimes there are plenty of side effects and relatively few benefits. And even when the side effects pose no danger, they may make people unbearably uncomfortable.

When a drug does work, the person taking it has to be under a doctor's care for as long as the therapy is continued, which is generally forever. Lowering cholesterol with drugs is like losing weight with drugs. When the drug is withdrawn, cholesterol returns.

Cholesterol drugs work by lowering cholesterol in one of two basic ways: Either they lower the amount of cholesterol-carrying LDLs or they increase the removal of cholesterol-rich bile acid.

All cholesterol drugs have adverse effects on a developing fetus. Therefore, none of these drugs can be taken by pregnant women.

GOING FOR THE LDL

Niacin

In the battle against high cholesterol, niacin has emerged as the weapon of preference. According to a government-sponsored panel of health experts, niacin is the first drug that a doctor should prescribe. It's a vitamin, after all, as well as a required nutrient and a "natural food." The only problem is that it has to be taken in unnaturally high doses.

Niacin works by inhibiting the flow of fatty acids to the liver. This leads to a decrease in the production of VLDL and triglycerides. Since LDL comes from VLDL, serum

LDL goes down. In doses that are high enough, niacin can reduce LDL by 20 to 30 percent. In some cases it can also raise HDL by as much as 10 to 15 percent.

Side Effects

Skin rashes and wheezing are sometimes bad enough to require medical attention. Common complaints are flushing, headache, diarrhea, dizziness, dry skin, nausea or vomiting, and stomach pain.

Niacin has to be carefully monitored in people with diabetes, glaucoma, gout, liver disease, or stomach ulcers.

Niacin interacts with chenodiol, isoniazid, and lovastatin.

Lovastatin (Mevacor ®)

Like niacin, lovastatin works in the liver. It has been shown to reduce LDL as much as 20 to 40 percent and raise HDL by about 10 percent.

Side Effects

There is a good deal of excitement about lovastatin. Of all the cholesterol-lowering drugs, this one causes the least discomfort. Ninety percent of the people who take it experience no adverse reactions.

For the unlucky 10 percent, medical attention is required when muscle pain or weakness is accompanied by fever or general malaise. Other complaints include constipation, diarrhea, flatulence, cramps, heartburn, nausea, muscle cramps and weakness, dizziness, headache, rash, blurred vision, and impairment of taste.

Lovastatin cannot be used by people with liver disease, and it must be carefully monitored in people prone to kidney failure.

This drug interacts with immunosuppressive drugs, gemfibrozil, and niacin.

Probucol (Lorelco ®)

Probucol is prescribed for hypercholesterolemics, whose cells cannot pull cholesterol from LDL. The drug changes the makeup of the LDL, making it more likely to be removed from the blood.

Probucol works best when it is taken with meals.

Side Effects

A few people suffer from chest pain, fainting, or swelling of the face, hands, feet, or mouth. These conditions warrant medical attention. Common complaints include bloating, diarrhea, nausea, vomiting, and stomach pain. Less common are dizziness, headache, and numbness.

Probucol cannot be used by people who have cirrhosis, and its use must be carefully monitored in people with gallstones, heart disease, liver disease, diabetes, or underactive thyroid.

This drug interacts with chenodiol.

BINDING UP THE BILE

All bile binders work by attaching themselves to bile acids in the intestines. The increased bulk prevents the bile from being reabsorbed; instead it is eliminated, forcing the liver to produce more. Since cholesterol is used to make bile, less cholesterol ends up going into the production of VLDL, and LDL levels go down.

Cholestyramine (Questran ®)

Cholestyramine comes in powder form. It must be carefully measured, mixed with a liquid, and given time to dissolve before being taken. If taken dry, cholestyramine will cause gagging.

Side Effects

Medical attention is required for severe constipation, black, tar-like stools, and severe stomach pain, nausea, or vomiting. Other complaints include heartburn, belching, bloating, and diarrhea.

Cholestyramine has to be carefully monitored in people with bleeding problems, constipation, diabetes, gallstones, heart disease, hemorrhoids, kidney disease, osteoporosis, stomach problems, or underactive thyroid.

This drug interacts with anticoagulants. It binds with chenodiol, digitalis, glycosides, and thyroid hormones. It impairs the absorption of diuretics, penicillin G, tetracyclines, vancomycin, and fat-soluble vitamins.

Colestipol (Colestid ®)

Like cholestyramine, colestipol is a powder that must be carefully measured, mixed with a liquid, and given time to dissolve before being taken.

Side Effects

Medical attention is required for severe constipation, severe stomach pain with nausea or vomiting, and unusual weight loss. Other complaints include belching, bloating, and diarrhea.

Colestipol cannot be taken by people with cirrhosis, and its use must be carefully monitored in people with bleeding disorders, constipation, heart disease, hemorrhoids, gallstones, gastrointestinal problems, or liver disease.

This drug interacts with anticoagulants. It binds with chenodiol, digitalis, glycosides, and thyroid hormones. It impairs the absorption of diuretics, penicillin G, tetracyclines, thiazide, vancomycin, and fat-soluble vitamins.

Clofibrate (Atromid-S®)

Clofibrate is a highly toxic drug. For this reason, it is used only for people with extremely elevated levels of serum cholesterol who do not respond to other drugs. When prescribed, it should be taken with food, which reduces the chance of its causing stomach distress.

Side Effects

Medical attention is required for blood in the urine, decrease in urination, painful urination, swelling of feet and lower legs, chest pain, shortness of breath, fever with chills or sore throat, irregular heartbeat, or severe stomach pain with nausea or vomiting. Other complaints include muscle aches or cramps, fatigue, decreased sexual ability, headache, weight gain, mouth sores, flatulence, and heart-burn.

Clofibrate cannot be used by people who have cirrhosis, and its use must be carefully monitored in people with gallstones, heart disease, hypothyroidism, kidney disease, liver disease, intestinal ulcers, or stomach ulcers.

This drug interacts with anticoagulants, antidiabetics, carbamazepine, chenodiol, chlorpropamide, desmopressin, diuretics, furosemide, lypressin, oral contraceptives, posterior pituitary medicines, probenecid, thiazide, and vasopressin.

ONE LAST WORD

It is a doctor, first and foremost, who determines when drugs are appropriate and which ones should be used. But it never hurts to be a knowledgeable consumer. Should drug therapy become necessary, know the options that are available. Then you can work with your doctor, providing necessary information and helping to make an educated decision.

Glossary _____

alpha-lipoprotein—high-density lipoprotein.

angina pectoris—sudden or periodic pain behind the breastbone or in the chest area around the heart. Angina pectoris is the result of the heart getting too little blood or oxygen.

arteriosclerosis—any disease that causes the walls of arteries to thicken and harden.

atherosclerosis—a disease of the walls of the arteries caused by the accumulation of lipids and other materials including blood products, fibrous tissue, and calcium.

beta-lipoprotein—low-density or very-low-density lipoprotein.

bile—a greenish-yellow fluid that contains large amounts of cholesterol. Bile is produced by the liver and serves to break up fats so that they can be absorbed and digested.

calorie—the amount of heat needed to raise the temperature of one kilogram of water one degree centigrade. When used in terms of food, calories refer to the heat-producing or energy-producing value in food when oxidized in the body.

cholesterol—a steroid alcohol present in all animal cells. Cholesterol is needed to determine the properties of cell membranes, to produce vitamin D, to produce progesterone and testosterone, and to make bile.

cholesterolemia—the presence of cholesterol in the blood.

coronary artery—one of the arteries leading to the heart.

diet (or dietary) cholesterol—cholesterol that is ingested with food.

fat—one of the basic types of foods. Fat, a particularly rich source of food energy, is found in both plant and animal foods in the form of glycerol combined with three fatty acids.

fatty acid—any of a number of carbon-, hydrogen-, and oxygen-containing molecules that combine with glycerol to form fat. Whether the fat is saturated, mono-unsaturated, or polyunsaturated depends on the number of double bonds between the carbon atoms and fatty acids present.

fatty streak—a small accumulation of fat within the wall of an artery. Fatty streaks are the first signs of the onset of atherosclerosis.

HDL—high-density lipoprotein.

high-density lipoprotein—a lipoprotein that contains more protein than lipid. High-density lipoprotein transports cholesterol away from tissues.

hydrogenation—the addition of hydrogen to the molecule of an unsaturated fatty acid.

hypercholesterolemia—a genetic disorder in which the body's cells are unable to pull low-density lipoproteins out of the bloodstream. Hypercholesterolemics have serum cholesterol levels above 300 milligrams per deciliter of blood and low-density lipoprotein levels above 200 milligrams per deciliter. Men with hypercholesterolemia often develop coronary heart disease in their thirties or forties. It is common for hypercholesterolemic women to develop coronary heart disease in their fifties or sixties.

hyperlipidemia—the presence of too much lipid in the bloodstream.

IDL—intermediate-density lipoprotein.

intermediate-density lipoprotein—the type of lipoprotein that remains when fat is removed from very-low-density lipoprotein. Intermediate-density lipoproteins are present in the blood for only a short time before they are taken up by the liver and transformed into low-density lipoprotein.

LDL—low-density lipoprotein.

lipid—a group of substances that are insoluble in water but that dissolve in ether. Lipids include fats, fatty acids, cholesterol and other sterols, and waxes.

lipoprotein—a lipid combined with a protein. The more protein there is compared to lipid, the denser the lipoprotein.

low-density lipoprotein—a lipoprotein that contains more lipid than protein. Low-density lipoprotein carries cholesterol through the blood and deposits it in tissues.

myocardial infarction—heart attack caused by the death of heart tissue when the blood supply to these muscle cells is too low to meet their needs.

monounsaturated fat—a fat in which the predominant number of fatty acids are missing two hydrogen atoms. In their place is a double bond between a pair of carbon atoms.

nutrient—a food that is used by the body for growth, repair, or maintenance.

oil—a fat that is liquid at room temperature. Oils are high in monounsaturated and polyunsaturated fatty acids.

plaque—fatty streaks within the walls of arteries that have, over time, absorbed cholesterol and other material such as fat, blood products, carbohydrates, and calcium.

polyunsaturated fat—a fat in which the predominant number of fatty acids present are missing two or more sets of double-bonded carbon atoms. In their place are two or more double bonds between carbon pairs.

saturated fat—a fat in which the predominant number of fatty acids are holding all the hydrogen they can.

serum cholesterol—cholesterol in the blood.

stroke—loss of consciousness, seizures, and local paralysis caused by hemorrhaging in the brain or by loss of oxygen due to the clogging of a cerebral blood vessel.

triglyceride—fat. Triglyceride is a compound of three fatty acids and glycerol, making it possible for the fatty acids to dissolve in water and therefore be transported through the blood.

very-low-density lipoprotein—the precursor of low-density lipoprotein. Very-low-density lipoproteins are made by the liver and contain mostly fat and cholesterol. After the fat is absorbed by body tissue, the lipoprotein exists for a short time as an intermediate-density lipoprotein. This material is removed from the bloodstream by the liver and turned into a low-density lipoprotein.

VLDL—very-low-density lipoprotein.

Equivalent Measures _____

3 teaspoons	= 1 tablespoon
4 tablespoons	= ¼ cup
1000 milligrams	= 1 gram

Liquid

2 tablespoons	= 1 fluid ounce
¼ cup	= 2 fluid ounces
½ cup	= 4 fluid ounces
1 cup	= 8 fluid ounces
2 cups	= 1 pint

Dry

4 ounces	= ¼ pound
16 ounces	= 1 pound

Abbreviations _____

C	cup
cal	calorie
fl oz	fluid ounce
g	gram
lb	pound
mg	milligram
NK	not known
oz	ounce
t	teaspoon
T	tablespoon
tr	trace
<	less than

GENERIC FOODS

	CAL	FAT (Cal)	CHOL (mg)
Abalone, fried, 3 oz	161	52	80
raw, 3 oz	89	6	72
Accent, 1 t	6	tr	0
Acerola, 1 C	31	3	0
Acerola juice, 1 C	51	7	0
Acorn squash, baked, ½ C cubes	57	1	0
boiled, ½ C mashed	41	1	0
raw, ½ C cubes	28	.5	0
Adzuki bean, boiled, ½ C	147	1	0
canned, sweetened, ½ C	351	.5	0
raw, ½ C	323	5	0
After-dinner mint, 1 oz	105	0	0
Agar, dried, 3.5 oz	306	3	0
raw, 3.5 oz	26	tr	0
Alfalfa sprouts, 1 C	10	2	0
Allspice, 1 t	5	2	0
Almond, slivers, 1 C	795	630	0
whole, 1 oz	165	135	0
Almond oil, 1 T	120	120	0
1 C	1927	1927	0
Amaranth, 1 C boiled	14	1	0
1 C raw	7	1	0
Anise seed, 1 t	7	3	0
Anisette, ⅔ fl oz	74	0	0
Apple, boiled, w/o skin, ½ C slices	46	3	0
canned, sweetened, ½ C slices	68	5	0
dehydrated, cooked, ½ C	71	1	0
uncooked, ½ C	104	2	0

58

	CAL	FAT (Cal)	CHOL (mg)
dried, cooked, sweetened, ½ C	116	1	0
cooked, unsweetened, ½ C	72	1	0
uncooked, 10 rings	155	2	0
frozen, unsweetened, heated, ½ C slices	48	3	0
microwaved, w/o skin, ½ C slices	48	3	0
raw, w/skin, 1	81	4	0
1 C	64	4	0
raw, w/o skin, 1	72	4	0
1 C	62	3	0
Apple juice, canned or bottled, 1 C	116	3	0
frozen concentrate, undiluted, 6 fl oz	349	7	0
frozen concentrate, diluted, 1 C	111	2	0
Applesauce, canned, sweetened, ½ C	97	2	0
canned, unsweetened, ½ C	53	.5	0
Apricot, canned in extra heavy syrup w/o skin,			
2 halves	87	.5	0
½ C	118	.5	0
in extra light syrup w/skin,			
3 halves	41	1	0
½ C	61	1	0
in heavy syrup w/skin,			
3 halves	70	1	0
½ C	107	1	0
in heavy syrup w/o skin,			
2 halves	75	1	0
½ C	107	1	0
in juice w/skin, 3 halves	40	tr	0
½ C	60	.5	0

	CAL	FAT (Cal)	CHOL (mg)
in light syrup w/skin,			
3 halves	54	.5	0
½ C	80	.5	0
in water w/skin, 3 halves	22	1	0
½ C	33	2	0
in water w/o skin, 2 halves	20	tr	0
½ C	26	tr	0
dehydrated, cooked, ½ C	156	3	0
uncooked, ½ C	192	3	0
dried, cooked, sweetened,			
½ C	153	tr	0
cooked, unsweetened,			
½ C	106	tr	0
uncooked, ½ C	160	3	0
frozen, sweetened, ½ C	119	1	0
raw, 3	51	4	0
raw, 1 C halves	74	5	0
Apricot brandy, ⅔ fl oz	64	0	0
Apricot kernel oil, 1 T	120	120	0
1 C	1927	1927	0
Apricot nectar, canned, 1 C	141	2	0
Arrowhead, boiled, 1 medium	9	tr	0
raw, 1 medium	12	tr	0
1 large	26	.5	0
Arrowroot, 1 T	29	0	0
Arrowroot cookie, 1	24	.8	tr
Artichoke, boiled, 1 medium	53	2	0
frozen, 3 oz	36	4	0
raw, 1 medium	65	2	0
1 large	83	3	0
Artichoke hearts, ½ C	37	1	0
Asparagus, boiled, 4 spears	15	2	0
½ C	22	3	0
canned, ½ C	17	2	0
frozen, 4 spears	17	2	0
3 oz	25	3	0
raw, 4 spears	13	1	0

	CAL	FAT (Cal)	CHOL (mg)
½ C	15	1	0
Asparagus bean, boiled, 1 pod	7	tr	0
½ C slices	25	.5	0
raw, 1 pod	6	.5	0
Au jus gravy, 1 can	48	5	1
2 T	5	.5	tr
dehydrated, 1 packet	79	30	4
prepared w/water, 1 C	19	7	1
Avocado, California, 1	306	270	0
1 C puree	407	359	0
Florida, 1 fruit	339	243	0
1 C puree	257	184	0
Babassu oil, 1 T	120	120	0
1 C	1927	1927	0
Baby food, apple blueberry, strained,			
1 jar (1 jar = 128 g/4.5 oz)	82	3	0
junior, 1 jar (1 junior = 213 g/7.5 oz)	137	4	0
apple-cherry juice, 1 jar	53	3	0
apple-grape juice, 1 jar	60	2	0
apple juice, 1 jar	61	1	0
apple-peach juice, 1 jar	55	1	0
apple-plum juice, 1 jar	63	0	0
apple-prune juice, 1 jar	94	2	0
apple raspberry, strained, 1 jar	79	2	0
junior, 1 jar	127	4	0
applesauce, strained, 1 jar	53	2	0
junior, 1 jar	79	0	0
applesauce & apricots, strained, 1 jar	60	3	0
junior, 1 jar	104	5	0
applesauce & cherries, strained, 1 jar	65	0	0
junior, 1 jar	106	0	0

	CAL	FAT (Cal)	CHOL (mg)
applesauce & pineapple, strained, 1 jar	48	1	0
junior, 1 jar	83	2	0
barley cereal, dry, 1 T	9	1	0
beef stew, toddler, 1 jar	90	19	22
beets, strained, 1 jar	43	1	0
carrots, strained, 1 jar	34	2	0
junior, 1 jar	67	4	0
cereal & eggs, strained, 1 jar	NK	17	66
cereal & egg yolks, strained, 1 jar	66	21	81
junior, 1 jar	110	34	132
chicken stew, toddler, 1 jar	132	58	49
egg yolks, strained, 1 jar	191	147	739
garden vegetables, strained, 1 jar	48	3	0
green beans, strained, 1 jar	32	1	0
junior, 1 jar	51	3	0
ham w/vegetables, junior, 1 jar	98	38	23
high protein cereal, dry, 1 T	9	1	0
w/apple & orange, 1 T	9	2	0
liver, strained, 1 jar	100	33	182
mixed fruit juice, 1 jar	61	1	0
mixed cereal, dry, 1 T	9	1	0
honey, 1 T	9	1	0
w/banana, 1 T	9	1	0
mixed vegetables, strained, 1 jar	52	5	0
junior, 1 jar	88	7	0
oatmeal, dry, 1 T	10	2	0
honey, dry, 1 T	9	2	0
w/banana, dry, 1 T	9	1	0
orange juice, 1 jar	58	3	0
orange-apple juice, 1 jar	56	3	0
orange-apple-banana juice, 1 jar	61	1	0

	CAL	FAT (Cal)	CHOL (mg)
orange-apricot juice, 1 jar	60	1	0
orange-banana juice, 1 jar	65	1	0
orange pineapple juice, 1 jar	63	1	0
peaches, strained, 1 jar	96	2	0
junior, 1 jar	157	4	0
pears, junior, 1 jar	93	2	0
pears & pineapple, strained, 1 jar	52	1	0
junior, 1 jar	93	4	0
peas, strained, 1 jar	52	4	0
pretzel, 1	24	1	0
prune-orange juice, 1 jar	91	4	0
rice cereal, dry, 1 T	9	1	0
honey, dry, 1 T	9	1	0
w/bananas, 1 T	10	1	0
squash, strained, 1 jar	30	2	0
junior, 1 jar	51	4	0
sweet potatoes, strained, 1 jar	77	2	0
junior, 1 jar	133	3	0
teething biscuit, 1	43	5	0
turkey & rice, strained, 1 jar	63	15	13
vegetables & bacon, strained, 1 jar	88	38	4
vegetables & ham, toddler, 1 jar	128	47	14
Bacon, 3 strips	110	81	16
Canadian, 2 strips	85	36	27
simulated, 1 strip	25	21	0
Bagel, 1	200	18	0
egg-type, 1	200	18	44
Baked beans, canned, vegetarian, ½ C	118	5	0
w/beef, ½ C	161	41	29
w/franks, ½ C	182	76	8
w/pork, ½ C	133	18	9

	CAL	FAT (Cal)	CHOL (mg)
w/pork & sweet sauce, ½ C	140	17	9
w/pork & tomato sauce, ½ C	123	12	9
home recipe, ½ C	190	58	6
Baking powder, 1 t	5	0	0
Balsam-pear, leafy tips, boiled, ½ C	10	.5	0
raw, ½ C	7	2	0
pods, boiled, ½ C	12	1	0
raw, ½ C	8	1	0
Bamboo shoots, boiled, ½ C slices	8	1	0
canned, ½ C slices	13	2	0
raw, ½ C slices	21	2	0
Banana, raw, 1	105	5	0
1 C mashed	207	10	0
dehydrated or powder, 1 T	21	1	0
Barbecue loaf, pork & beef, 1 slice, 1/16″	40	18	9
1 oz	49	23	11
Barbecue sauce, 1 C	188	41	0
Barley, 1 T	28	1	0
1 C	401	17	0
pearled, light, uncooked, 1 C	700	18	0
Basil, dried, 1 t	3	tr	0
Bass, freshwater, raw, 3 oz	97	28	58
striped, raw, 3 oz	82	18	68
Bay leaf, 1	5	tr	0
Bean w/bacon soup, condensed, 1 C	420	130	6
prepared w/water, 1 C	173	53	3
dehydrated, 1 packet	105	19	3
Bean w/frankfurter soup, condensed, 1 C	454	152	29
prepared w/water, 1 C	187	63	12
Bean w/ham soup, chunky, 1 C	231	77	22
Beef, 3 oz			
brain, pan fried	167	121	1696
raw	108	24	1422

	CAL	FAT (Cal)	CHOL (mg)
simmered	136	96	1746
bottom round, choice, lean, braised	191	76	81
choice, lean & fat, braised	224	116	81
choice, lean, raw	129	48	51
choice, lean & fat, raw	192	119	54
good, lean, braised	182	67	81
good, lean & fat, braised	215	106	81
good, lean, raw	123	45	51
good, lean & fat, raw	192	121	54
prime, lean, braised	212	97	81
prime, lean & fat, braised	253	146	81
prime, lean, raw	135	56	51
prime, lean & fat, raw	192	118	54
brisket, flat half, lean, braised	223	121	77
flat half, lean & fat, braised	347	267	78
flat half, lean, raw	147	74	54
flat half, lean & fat, raw	300	242	22
point half, lean, braised	181	66	81
point half, lean & fat, braised	311	221	81
point half, lean, raw	114	37	51
point half, lean & fat, raw	252	187	60
whole, lean, braised	205	198	79
whole, lean & fat, braised	332	248	79
whole, lean, raw	132	56	51
whole, lean & fat, raw	276	215	63
chuck, blade roast, choice, lean, braised	234	121	90
blade roast, choice, lean & fat, braised	330	237	87
blade roast, choice, lean, raw	144	73	54
blade roast, choice, lean & fat, raw	246	187	63

	CAL	FAT (Cal)	CHOL (mg)
blade roast, good, lean, braised	218	105	90
blade roast, good, lean & fat, braised	311	217	88
blade roast, good, lean, raw	129	59	54
blade roast, good, lean & fat, raw	222	159	60
blade roast, prime, lean, braised	270	157	90
blade roast, prime, lean & fat, braised	354	261	87
blade roast, prime, lean, raw	174	103	54
blade roast, prime, lean & fat, raw	279	219	63
pot roast, choice, lean, braised	199	79	85
pot roast, choice, lean & fat, braised	301	206	84
pot roast, choice, lean, raw	117	39	51
pot roast, choice, lean & fat, raw	222	157	60
pot roast, good, lean, braised	189	69	85
pot roast, good, lean & fat, braised	287	187	84
pot roast, good, lean, raw	111	33	51
pot roast, good, lean & fat, raw	201	134	57
pot roast, prime, lean, braised	222	103	85
pot roast, prime, lean & fat, braised	332	237	84
pot roast, prime, lean, raw	132	53	51

	CAL	FAT (Cal)	CHOL (mg)
pot roast, prime lean & fat, raw	249	185	60
eye round, choice, lean, raw	114	34	45
choice, lean & fat, raw	171	33	51
choice, lean, roasted	53	51	59
choice, lean & fat, roasted	207	110	62
good, lean, raw	108	28	45
good, lean & fat, raw	159	87	51
good, lean, roasted	151	45	59
good, lean & fat, roasted	201	104	62
prime, lean, raw	126	47	45
prime, lean & fat, raw	189	115	51
prime, lean, roasted	168	63	59
prime, lean & fat, roasted	213	114	61
flank, choice, lean, braised	208	105	60
choice, lean & fat, braised	218	118	61
choice, lean, broiled	207	114	60
choice, lean & fat, broiled	216	125	60
choice, lean, raw	144	72	42
choice, lean & fat, raw	165	96	45
ground, extra lean, raw (4 oz)	265	173	78
baked, medium	213	123	70
baked, well done	232	122	91
broiled, medium	217	125	71
broiled, well done	225	121	84
pan fried, medium	216	126	69
pan fried, well done	224	122	79
ground, lean, raw (4 oz)	298	210	85
baked, medium	227	140	66
baked, well done	248	140	84
broiled, medium	231	141	74
broiled, well done	238	135	86
pan fried, medium	234	146	71
pan fried, well done	235	135	81
ground beef, regular, raw (4 oz)	351	270	96

	CAL	FAT (Cal)	CHOL (mg)
baked, medium	244	160	74
baked, well done	269	164	92
broiled, medium	246	158	76
broiled, well done	248	149	86
pan fried, medium	260	173	75
pan fried, well done	243	145	83
ground patties, frozen, raw			
(4 oz)	319	236	89
broiled, medium	240	150	80
heart, raw	99	29	120
simmered	148	43	164
kidneys, raw	90	23	81
simmered	122	26	329
liver, braised	137	37	331
pan fried	184	61	410
raw	120	29	300
lungs, braised	102	28	236
raw	78	19	69
porterhouse steak, choice,			
lean, broiled	185	83	68
choice, lean & fat, broiled	254	162	70
choice, lean, raw	135	60	51
choice, lean & fat, raw	243	178	60
rib, whole, choice, lean,			
broiled	198	104	69
whole, choice, lean & fat,			
broiled	313	234	73
whole, choice, lean, raw	144	70	51
whole, choice, lean & fat,			
raw	288	229	60
whole, choice, lean,			
roasted	209	109	68
whole, choice, lean & fat,			
roasted	328	248	72
whole, good, lean, broiled	181	86	69
whole, good, lean & fat,			
broiled	289	210	72

	CAL	FAT (Cal)	CHOL (mg)
whole, good, lean, raw	129	58	51
whole, good, lean & fat, raw	264	204	60
whole, good, lean, roasted	191	93	68
whole, good, lean & fat, roasted	306	75	72
whole, prime, lean, broiled	238	143	69
whole, prime, lean & fat, broiled	347	269	73
whole, prime, lean, raw	174	103	51
whole, prime, lean & fat, raw	315	257	63
whole, prime, lean, roasted	248	149	68
whole, prime, lean & fat, roasted	361	282	73
rib, large end, choice, lean, broiled	203	114	70
large end, choice, lean & fat, broiled	327	253	74
large end, choice, lean, raw	147	76	51
large end, choice, lean & fat, raw	313	246	63
large end, choice, lean, roasted	210	110	68
large end, choice, lean & fat, roasted	316	233	72
large end, good, lean, broiled	183	93	70
large end, good, lean & fat, broiled	301	226	73
large end, good, lean, raw	135	63	51
large end, good, lean & fat, raw	279	221	60

	CAL	FAT (Cal)	CHOL (mg)
large end, good, lean, roasted	197	97	68
large end, good, lean & fat, roasted	304	220	72
large end, prime, lean, broiled	250	160	70
large end, prime, lean & fat, broiled	361	96	74
large end, prime, lean, raw	180	108	51
large end, prime, lean & fat, raw	327	269	63
large end, prime, lean, roasted	241	140	68
large end, prime, lean & fat, roasted	346	265	72
rib, small end, choice, lean, broiled	191	89	68
small end, choice, lean & fat, broiled	282	195	71
small end, choice, lean, raw	138	66	51
small end, choice, lean & fat, raw	267	205	60
small end, choice, lean, roasted	206	109	68
small end, choice, lean & fat, roasted	312	231	72
small end, good, lean, broiled	178	76	68
small end, good, lean & fat, broiled	263	175	71
small end, good, lean, raw	126	51	51
small end, good, lean & fat, raw	243	180	60
small end, good, lean, roasted	183	86	68

	CAL	FAT (Cal)	CHOL (mg)
small end, good, lean & fat roasted	283	201	72
small end, prime, lean, broiled	221	124	68
small end, prime, lean & fat, broiled	309	223	71
small end, prime, lean, raw	171	97	51
small end, prime, lean & fat, raw	297	237	60
small end, prime, lean, roasted	259	163	68
small end, prime, lean & fat, roasted	357	277	72
rib eye, small end, choice, lean, broiled	191	267	68
small end, choice, lean & fat, broiled	250	158	70
small end, choice, lean, raw	138	65	51
small end, choice, lean & fat, raw	213	147	57
round, full cut, choice, lean, broiled	53	61	70
full cut, choice, lean & fat, broiled	233	140	71
full cut, choice, lean, raw	62	38	48
full cut, choice, lean & fat, raw	204	134	57
full cut, good, lean, broiled	157	53	70
full cut, good, lean & fat, broiled	222	129	71
full cut, good, lean, raw	114	33	48
full cut, good, lean & fat, raw	195	125	57

	CAL	FAT (Cal)	CHOL (mg)
shank crosscuts, choice,			
lean, raw	108	29	33
choice, lean & fat, raw	135	59	36
choice, lean, simmered	171	49	66
choice, lean & fat,			
simmered	208	93	67
shortribs, choice, lean,			
braised	251	138	79
choice, lean & fat, braised	400	321	80
choice, lean, raw	147	78	51
choice, lean & fat, raw	330	277	66
sirloin, choice, lean, broiled	180	69	76
choice, lean & fat, broiled	240	141	77
choice, lean, pan fried	202	84	85
choice, lean & fat, pan			
fried	288	188	84
choice, lean, raw	117	40	51
choice, lean & fat, raw	225	158	60
good, lean, broiled	170	60	76
good lean & fat, broiled	232	133	77
good, lean, raw	111	34	51
good, lean & fat, raw	210	142	60
prime, lean, broiled	201	91	76
prime, lean & fat, broiled	271	174	77
prime, lean, raw	132	54	51
prime, lean & fat, raw	246	182	60
spleen, braised	123	32	295
raw	90	23	75
suet, raw	726	720	57
T-bone steak, choice, lean,			
broiled	182	79	68
choice, lean & fat, broiled	276	188	71
choice, lean, raw	135	62	51
choice, lean & fat, raw	261	200	60
tenderloin, choice, lean,			
broiled	176	73	72
choice, lean & fat, broiled	230	136	73

	CAL	FAT (Cal)	CHOL (mg)
choice, lean, raw	126	52	54
choice, lean & fat, raw	209	141	59
choice, lean, roasted	189	89	73
choice, lean & fat, roasted	262	173	74
good, lean, broiled	167	64	72
good, lean & fat, broiled	216	120	73
good, lean, raw	120	45	54
good, lean & fat, raw	196	128	59
good, lean, roasted	177	77	73
good, lean & fat, roasted	245	155	74
prime, lean, broiled	197	95	72
prime, lean & fat, broiled	270	179	73
prime, lean, raw	144	68	54
prime, lean & fat, raw	245	180	60
prime, lean, roasted	217	117	73
prime, lean & fat, roasted	305	219	75
tip round, choice, lean, raw	114	35	51
choice lean & fat, raw	180	108	54
choice, lean, roasted	164	178	69
choice, lean & fat, roasted	216	120	70
good, lean, raw	108	29	51
good, lean & fat, raw	165	94	54
good, lean, roasted	156	154	69
good, lean & fat, roasted	205	108	70
prime, lean, raw	123	47	51
prime, lean & fat, raw	192	123	57
prime, lean, roasted	181	77	69
prime, lean & fat, roasted	242	147	71
thymus, braised	271	191	250
raw	201	156	189
tongue, simmered	241	159	91
raw	189	123	75
top loin, choice, lean, broiled	176	72	65
choice, lean & fat, broiled	243	150	68
choice, lean, raw	132	53	51
choice, lean & fat, raw	246	180	59
good, lean, broiled	162	58	65

	CAL	FAT (Cal)	CHOL (mg)
good, lean & fat, broiled	223	128	67
good, lean, raw	117	40	51
good, lean & fat, raw	224	157	58
prime, lean, broiled	208	104	65
prime, lean & fat, broiled	288	198	68
prime, lean, raw	159	27	51
prime, lean & fat, raw	274	209	59
top round, choice, lean, broiled	165	49	72
choice, lean & fat, broiled	181	69	72
choice, lean, pan fried	193	66	83
choice, lean & fat, pan fried	246	131	82
choice, lean, raw	114	32	48
choice, lean & fat, raw	147	69	51
good, lean, broiled	156	42	72
good, lean & fat, broiled	176	64	72
good, lean, raw	108	26	48
good, lean & fat, raw	141	61	51
prime, lean, broiled	183	68	72
prime, lean & fat, broiled	201	89	72
prime, lean, raw	132	47	48
prime, lean & fat, raw	159	81	51
tripe, raw	84	30	27
Beef & vegetable stew, home recipe, 1 C	220	99	71
Beef broth or bouillon, 1 C	16	5	tr
dehydrated, 1 packet	14	5	1
dehydrated, 1 cube	6	1	tr
Beef gravy, 1 can	155	62	9
1 T	16	6	1
Beef mushroom soup, condensed, 1 can	NK	126	15
prepared w/water, 1 C	NK	52	7
Beef noodle, condensed, 1 can	204	67	12
prepared w/water, 1 C	84	28	5
dehydrated, 1 packet	30	5	1

	CAL	FAT (Cal)	CHOL (mg)
Beef potpie, home recipe, ⅓ of 9" pie	515	270	42
Beef soup, chunky, 1 C	171	46	14
Beef tallow, 1 T	116	115	14
1 C	1849	1849	223
Beer, regular, 12 fl oz	150	0	0
light, 12 fl oz	95	0	0
Beerwurst, beef, 1 slice, ⅛"	76	62	14
pork, 1 slice, ⅛"	55	39	13
Beet, boiled, ½ C slices	26	.5	0
canned, ½ C slices	27	1	0
Harvard, canned, ½ C	89	.5	0
pickled, ½ C	75	1	0
raw, ½ C slices	30	1	0
Beet greens, boiled, ½ C	20	1	0
raw, ½ C	4	tr	0
Benedictine, ⅔ fl oz	69	0	0
Berliner, pork & beef, 1 slice, ⅛"	53	36	11
1 oz	65	44	13
Bernaise sauce, dehydrated, 1 packet	90	20	tr
prepared w/whole milk & butter, 1 C	701	615	189
Biscuit, from mix, 1 biscuit	95	21	tr
from refrigerated dough, 1 biscuit	65	18	1
home recipe, 1 biscuit	100	45	tr
Black bean, boiled, ½ C	113	4	0
raw, ½ C	330	12	0
Black bean soup, condensed, 1 can	285	37	0
prepared w/water, 1 C	116	14	0
Black-eyed pea, boiled, ½ C	95	5	0
immature seed, boiled, ½ C	90	5	0
frozen, ½ C	113	5	0
Black pepper, 1 t	9	tr	0
Black turtle soup beans, boiled, ½ C	120	3	0
canned, ½ C	109	3	0
raw, ½ C	312	7	0

	CAL	FAT (Cal)	CHOL (mg)
Blackberry, canned in heavy syrup, ½ C	118	2	0
frozen, sweetened, ½ C	49	6	0
raw, ½ C	37	3	0
Blueberry, canned in heavy syrup, ½ C	56	2	0
frozen, sweetened, ½ C	94	1	0
frozen, unsweetened, ½ C	39	4	0
raw, ½ C	41	2	0
Bluefish, raw, 3 oz	105	32	50
Blood sausage, 1 oz	107	88	34
Bologna, beef, 1 slice, ⅛"	88	72	16
beef & pork, 1 slice, ⅛"	89	89	16
pork, 1 slice, ⅛"	70	51	17
turkey, 1 slice	113	78	56
Borage, boiled, 3.5 oz	25	7	0
raw, ½ C	9	3	0
Boysenberry, canned in heavy syrup, ½ C	113	1	0
frozen, unsweetened, ½ C	33	2	0
Bratwurst, 1 link	256	198	51
Braunschweiger, 1 slice, ¼"	56	52	28
Brazil nut, shelled, 1 C	185	171	0
Bread, Boston brown, 1 slice	95	9	3
cracked wheat, 1 slice	65	9	0
dinner roll, commercial, 1	85	18	tr
home recipe, 1	120	27	12
English muffin, 1	140	9	0
frankfurter roll, 1	115	18	tr
French, 1 slice, 5"	100	9	0
hamburger bun, 1	115	18	tr
hard roll, 1	155	18	tr
hoagie, 1	400	72	tr
Italian, 1 slice,	85	tr	0
mixed grain, 1 slice	65	9	0
oatmeal, 1 slice	65	9	0
pita, 1	165	9	0

	CAL	FAT (Cal)	CHOL (mg)
pumpernickel, 1 slice	80	9	0
raisin, 1 slice	65	9	0
rye, 1 slice	65	9	0
submarine, 1	400	72	tr
wheat, 1 slice	65	9	0
white, 1 slice	65	9	0
cubes, 1 C	80	9	0
whole wheat, 1 slice	70	9	0
Vienna, 1 slice	70	9	0
Breadcrumbs, dry, ¼ C	98	11	1
soft, ¼ C	30	4	0
Breadfruit, raw, ¼ small fruit	99	2	0
Breakfast strips, beef, raw, 3 slices	276	237	56
cooked, 3 slices	153	105	40
Broad bean, boiled, 3.5 oz	56	5	0
raw, 1 bean	6	.5	0
½ C	40	3	0
Broad bean seed, boiled, ½ C	93	3	0
canned, ½ C	91	3	0
raw, ½ C	256	10	0
Broccoli, boiled, 1 spear	53	5	0
½ C	23	2	0
frozen, chopped, ½ C	25	1	0
spears, ½ C	25	1	0
raw, 1 spear	42	5	0
½ C	12	1	0
Brotwurst, 1 link	226	175	44
Brown gravy, dehydrated, 1 packet	85	18	2
prepared w/water, 1 C	9	2	tr
Brussels sprout, boiled, ½ C	30	4	0
frozen, ½ C	33	3	0
raw, ½ C	19	1	0
Buckwheat flour, dark, 1 C	333	23	0
light, 1 C	347	11	0
Bulgar, uncooked, 1 C	600	21	0
Burbot, raw, 3 oz	76	6	51
Burdock root, boiled, 1 root	146	2	0

	CAL	FAT (Cal)	CHOL (mg)
½ C pieces	55	10	0
raw, 1 root	112	2	0
½ C pieces	43	1	0
Butter, 1 pat	36	36	11
1 T	100	100	31
1 stick	813	813	248
anhydrous oil, 1 C	1795	1795	524
1 T	112	112	33
whipped, 1 pat	27	27	8
1 stick	542	542	165
Butterbur, boiled, 3.5 oz	8	tr	0
canned, 1 C	3	1	0
raw, 1 C	13	.5	0
Butterfish, raw 3 oz	124	61	55
Butternut squash, baked, ½ C cubes	41	1	0
frozen, ½ C mashed	47	1	0
raw, ½ C cubes	32	.5	0
Cabbage, boiled, ½ C shredded	16	2	0
raw, ½ C shredded	8	.5	0
Cake, angel food, ¹⁄₁₂ of 9.75″ tube cake	125	tr	0
brownie w/nuts, home recipe, 1	95	54	18
w/nuts & frosting, commercial, 1	100	36	14
carrot cake w/cream cheese frosting, ¹⁄₁₆ of 10″ tube cake	365	189	74
cheesecake, ¹⁄₁₂ of 9″ cake	280	162	170
crumb coffeecake, ⅙ of 7″ × 5″ cake	230	63	47
devil's food w/chocolate frosting, ¹⁄₁₆ of 2 layer cake	235	72	37
1 cupcake	120	36	19

	CAL	FAT (Cal)	CHOL (mg)
devil's food snack cake w/ creme filling, 1	105	36	15
fruitcake, dark, ⅔" arc	165	63	20
gingerbread, ⅑ of 8" × 8" cake	175	36	1
pound cake, 1/17 of loaf, homemade,	120	45	32
commercial	110	45	64
sheet cake, ⅑ of 9" × 9" cake	315	108	61
w/uncooked white frosting	445	126	70
sponge snack cake w/creme filling, 1	155	45	7
white cake w/white frosting, 1/16 of 2 layer cake, commercial	260	81	3
yellow w/chocolate frosting, 1/16 of 2 layer cake, homemade	235	72	36
commercial	245	99	38
Candy corn, 1 oz	105	0	0
Cantaloupe, ½	94	7	0
1 C cubes	57	4	0
Carambola, 1	42	4	0
Caramel, plain or chocolate, 1 oz	115	27	1
Caraway seed, 1 t	8	.5	0
Cardamon seed, 1 t	6	0	0
Cardoon, boiled, 3.5 oz	22	1	0
raw, ½ C shredded	18	1	0
Carissa, 1 fruit	12	2	0
Carob flour, 1 T	14	.5	0
1 C	185	6	0
Carp, broiled, 3 oz	138	55	72
raw, 3 oz	108	43	56
Carrot, boiled, ½ C slices	35	1	0
canned, ½ C slices	17	1	0
frozen, ½ C slices	26	1	0

	CAL	FAT (Cal)	CHOL (mg)
raw, 1 carrot	31	1	0
½ C shredded	24	1	0
Carrot juice, canned, ½ C	49	2	0
Casaba melon, ¹⁄₁₀	43	1	0
1 C cubed	45	2	0
Cashew nut, dry roasted, 1 C	785	567	0
1 oz	165	117	0
roasted in oil, 1 C	750	567	0
1 oz	165	126	0
Cassava, raw, 3.5 oz	120	4	0
Cassava flour, 1 C	320	5	0
Catfish, breaded & fried, 3 oz	194	102	69
raw, 3 oz	99	33	49
Catjang cowpea, boiled, ½ C	100	5	0
raw, ½ C	288	16	0
Catsup, 1 T	15	tr	0
Cauliflower, boiled, ½ C pieces	15	1	0
frozen, ½ C pieces	17	2	0
raw, ½ C pieces	12	1	0
Cauliflower soup, dehydrated, 1 packet	68	15	tr
Caviar, black, 1 T	40	26	94
red, 1 T	40	26	94
Celeriac, boiled, 3.5 oz	25	2	0
raw, ½ C	31	2	0
Celery, boiled, ½ C diced	11	1	0
raw, 1 stalk	6	.5	0
½ C diced	9	.5	0
Celery seed, 1 t	11	.5	0
Celtuce, raw, 1 leaf	2	tr	0
Cervelat, beef & pork, 1 slice, ⅛"	80	62	16
Chayote, boiled, ½ C pieces	19	3	0
raw, 1	49	5	0
½ C pieces	16	2	0
Cheese, American, pasteurized processed, 1 oz	105	81	27
cheese food, 1 oz	95	63	18

	CAL	FAT (Cal)	CHOL (mg)
cheese food, cold pack, 1 oz	94	50	18
cheese spread, 1 oz	80	54	16
pimento cheese, 1 oz	66	47	16
blue, 1 oz	100	72	21
brick, 1 oz	105	72	27
Brie, 1 oz	95	NK	28
Camembert, 1 oz	85	58	20
cheddar, 1 oz	115	83	30
1 C shredded	455	333	119
Cheshire, 1 oz	110	NK	29
Colby, 1 oz	68	47	16
cottage, creamed, large curd, 1 C	235	90	34
creamed, small curd, 1 C	215	81	31
low-fat (2%), 1 C	205	37	19
low-fat (1%), 1 C	164	20	10
uncreamed (<.5% fat), 1 C	125	9	10
cream, 1 oz	100	90	31
Edam, 1 oz	101	67	25
feta, 1 oz	75	54	25
fontina, 1 oz	110	75	33
gjetost, 1 oz	132	71	NK
Gouda, 1 oz	101	66	32
Gruyere, 1 oz	117	75	31
Limburger, 1 oz	93	66	26
mozzarella, whole milk, 1 oz	80	54	22
whole milk, low moisture, 1 oz	90	60	25
part skim milk, 1 oz	72	38	16
part skim, low moisture, 1 oz	79	41	15
Muenster, 1 oz	105	81	27
Neufchatel, 1 oz	74	57	22
Parmesan, 1 oz	130	81	22
grated, 1 T	25	18	4

	CAL	FAT (Cal)	CHOL (mg)
Port du Salut, 1 oz	100	68	35
provolone, 1 oz	100	72	20
ricotta, whole milk, 1 C	430	288	124
part skim milk, 1 C	340	171	76
Romano, 1 oz	110	NK	29
Roquefort, 1 oz	105	65	26
Swiss, 1 oz	105	72	26
pasteurized processed, 1 oz	95	63	24
pasteurized processed cheese food, 1 oz	92	NK	23
Tilsit, whole milk, 1 oz	96	63	29
Cheese sauce, dehydrated, 1 packet	158	81	18
prepared w/whole milk, 1 C	307	154	53
Cheese soup, condensed, 1 can	377	229	72
prepared w/whole milk, 1 C	230	131	48
prepared w/water, 1 C	155	94	30
Cheeseburger, 1	300	1356	44
¼ lb patty	525	279	104
Cheesefurter, 1	141	112	29
Cherimoya, 1	515	20	0
Cherry, sour, red, raw, 1 C w/pits	51	3	0
canned in extra heavy syrup, ½ C	148	1	0
in heavy syrup, ½ C	116	1	0
in light syrup, ½ C	94	1	0
in water, ½ C	43	1	0
frozen, unsweetened, ½ C	36	6	0
raw, 1 C seeded	77	4	0
sweet, canned in extra heavy syrup, ½ C	133	2	0
in heavy syrup, ½ C	107	2	0
in juice, ½ C	68	tr	0
in light syrup, ½ C	85	2	0
in water, ½ C	57	1	0
frozen, sweetened, ½ C	116	2	0
raw, 10	49	6	0

	CAL	FAT (Cal)	CHOL (mg)
1 C	104	13	0
Chervil, ¼ C	28	4	0
Chestnut, roasted, shelled, 1 C	350	27	0
Chestnut flour, 1 C	362	33	0
Chicken, canned, boneless, 5 oz	235	99	88
fried, batter dipped, light meat,			
½ breast	365	162	119
dark meat, 1 drumstick	195	99	62
fried, flour coated, light meat,			
½ breast	220	81	87
dark meat, 1 drumstick	120	63	44
liver, cooked, 1	30	9	126
roasted, w/o skin, light meat,			
½ breast	140	27	73
dark meat, 1 drumstick	75	18	41
stewed, flesh only, light & dark meat,			
1 cup chopped	250	81	116
Chicken a la king, home recipe, 1 C	470	306	221
Chicken & dumpling soup,			
condensed, 1 can	236	121	80
prepared w/water, 1 C	97	50	34
Chicken & noodles, home recipe,			
1 C	365	162	103
Chicken broth, condensed, 1 can	94	29	3
prepared w/water 1 C	39	13	1
dehydrated, 1 packet	16	7	1
dehydrated, 1 cube	9	2	0
Chicken chow mein, canned, 1 C	95	tr	8
home recipe, 1 C	255	90	75
Chicken fat, 1 T	115	115	11
1 C	1846	1846	174
Chicken frankfurter, 1	115	81	45
Chicken gravy, 1 can	236	153	6
2 T	24	15	.5

	CAL	FAT (Cal)	CHOL (mg)
dehydrated, 1 C prepared	83	17	2
Chicken gumbo, condensed, 1 can	137	31	9
prepared w/water, 1 C	56	13	5
Chicken mushroom soup, condensed, 1 can	NK	200	24
prepared w/water, 1 C	NK	82	10
Chicken noodle soup, chunky, 1 C	NK	54	18
condensed, 1 can	182	50	15
prepared w/water, 1 C	75	22	7
dehydrated, 1 packet	38	7	2
w/meatballs, 1 C	99	32	10
Chicken potpie, home recipe, ⅓ of 9″ pie	545	279	56
Chicken rice soup, chunky, 1 C	286	65	27
condensed, 1 can	146	42	15
prepared w/water, 1 C	60	17	7
dehydrated, 1 packet	60	13	3
Chicken roll, light meat, 2 slices	90	38	28
Chicken soup, chunky, 1 C	178	60	30
Chicken vegetable soup, chunky 1 C	167	43	17
condensed, 1 can	181	62	21
prepared w/water, 1 C	74	26	10
dehydrated, 1 packet	37	5	2
Chickpea, boiled, ½ C	134	19	0
canned, ½ C	143	12	0
raw, ½ C	364	54	0
Chicory greens, raw, ½ C chopped	21	2	0
Chicory roots, raw, ½ C pieces	33	1	0
Chili beef soup, condensed, 1 can	411	144	32
prepared w/water, 1 C	169	59	12
Chili con carne w/beans, canned, 1 C	340	144	28
Chili pepper, hot, canned, 1 pepper	18	.5	0
½ C chopped	17	.5	0
dried, 1 t ground	9	tr	0
raw, 1 pepper	18	1	0
½ C chopped	30	1	0

	CAL	FAT (Cal)	CHOL (mg)
Chili w/beans, canned, ½ C	144	63	22
Chinese preserving melon, boiled,			
½ C cubes	11	2	0
raw, 1 C cubes	17	2	0
Chinese radish, boiled, ½ C slices	13	2	0
dried, ½ C	157	4	0
raw, 1 radish	62	3	0
½ C slices	8	tr	0
Chipped beef, 2 oz	145	36	46
Chive, freeze-dried, 1 T		tr	0
raw, 1 T	1	tr	0
Chocolate, baking, 1 oz	141	133	0
dark, 1 oz	150	90	0
flavored syrup, thin, 2 T	85	tr	0
fudge type, 2 T	125	45	0
milk, 1 oz	145	81	54
w/almonds, 1 oz	150	90	45
w/peanuts, 1 oz	155	99	45
w/rice cereal, 1 oz	140	63	54
semisweet, small pieces, 1 C			
or 6 oz	860	61	0
Chop suey w/beef & pork, home			
recipe, 1 C	300	153	68
Chopped beef, smoked, 2 slices	75	23	26
Chow mein noodle, canned, 1 C	220	99	5
Chrysanthemum, boiled, ½ C pieces	10	.5	0
raw, 1 stem	2	tr	0
Cinnamon, ground, 1 t	6	0	0
Cisco, smoked, 3 oz	151	91	27
Clam, breaded & fried, 20 small	376	189	115
canned, 3 oz	126	15	57
cooked, moist heat, 20 small	133	16	60
3 oz	126	15	57
raw, 9 large or 20 small	133	11	60
3 oz	63	7	29
Clam chowder, Manhattan, chunky,			
1 C	133	30	14

	CAL	FAT (Cal)	CHOL (mg)
Manhattan, condensed, 1 can	187	48	6
prepared w/water, 1 C	78	21	2
dehydrated, 1 C prepared	65	14	0
New England, condensed, 1 can	214	55	12
prepared w/whole milk, 1 C	163	59	22
prepared w/water, 1 C	95	26	5
dehydrated, 1 C prepared	95	33	1
Clove, ground, 1 t	7	tr	0
Cocoa butter, 1 T	120	120	0
1 C	1927	1927	0
Coconut, dried, sweetened, 1 C shredded	470	297	0
raw, 2″ × 2″ piece	160	135	0
shredded or grated, 1 C	285	243	0
Coconut oil, 1 T	120	120	0
1 C	1927	1927	0
Cod, Atlantic, canned, 3 oz	89	7	47
cooked, dry heat, 3 oz	89	7	47
dried & salted, 3 oz	246	18	129
raw, 3 oz	70	5	37
Pacific, raw, 3 oz	70	5	31
Coffee, brewed, 6 fl oz	tr	0	0
instant, 6 fl oz	tr	0	0
Cognac, ⅔ fl oz	75	0	0
Cole slaw, ½ C	42	14	0
Collards, boiled, ½ C chopped	13	1	0
frozen, ½ C chopped	31	3	0
raw, ½ C chopped	18	2	0
Consomme w/gelatin, condensed, 1 can	71	0	0
prepared w/water, 1 C	29	0	0
dehydrated, 1 packet	77	.5	0
prepared w/water, 1 C	17	tr	0
Cookie, chocolate chip, commercial, 4	180	81	5

	CAL	FAT (Cal)	CHOL (mg)
home recipe, 4	185	99	18
refrigerated dough, 4	225	99	22
fig bar, 4	210	36	27
oatmeal w/raisins, 4	245	90	18
peanut butter, home recipe, 4	245	126	22
sandwich cookies, chocolate, 4	195	72	0
vanilla, 4	195	72	0
shortbread, commercial, 4 small	155	72	27
home recipe, 2 large	145	72	0
sugar, refrigerated dough, 4	235	108	29
vanilla wafers, 10	185	63	25
Coriander, dried, 1 t ground	3	1	0
raw, ¼ C	1	tr	0
Coriander seed, 1 t	6	tr	0
Corn, boiled, 1 ear	83	9	0
½ C	89	9	0
canned, ½ C	66	7	0
vacuum packed, ½ C	83	5	0
creamed, canned, ½ C	93	5	0
frozen, 1 ear	59	4	0
boiled, ½ C	67	.5	0
raw, 1 ear	77	9	0
½ C	66	8	0
w/red & green peppers, canned, ½ C	86	.5	0
Corn chip, 1 oz	155	81	0
Corn flour, 1 C	405	26	0
Corn meal, whole-ground, 1 C	435	45	0
bolted, 1 C	440	36	0
de-germed, dry, 1 C	500	18	0
de-germed, cooked, 1 C	120	tr	0
Corn oil, 1 T	120	120	0
1 C	1927	1927	0
Corn pudding, 1 C	271	120	230
Corn syrup, 2 T	122	0	0

	CAL	FAT (Cal)	CHOL (mg)
Corned beef, brisket, raw, 3 oz	168	114	45
brisket, cooked, 3 oz	213	145	83
canned, 1 slice	53	28	18
jellied loaf, 2 slices	87	31	27
Cornsalad, raw, ½ C	6	1	0
Cottonseed flour, 1 C	356	59	0
Cottonseed oil, 1 T	120	120	0
1 C	1927	1927	0
Cowpea, boiled, ½ C	100	4	0
canned, ½ C	92	6	0
w/pork, ½ C	99	17	8
frozen, ½ C	112	5	0
raw, ½ C	283	9	0
Cowpea leafy tips, boiled, ½ C chopped	6	tr	0
raw, 1 leaf	1	tr	0
½ C chopped	5	1	0
Cowpea pod, boiled, ½ C	16	1	0
raw, 1 pod	5	.5	0
½ C	21	1	0
Crab, Alaskan King, cooked, moist heat, 1 leg	129	19	72
imitation, 3 oz	87	10	17
raw, 1 leg	144	9	72
blue, canned, 3 oz	84	9	76
crab cake, 1 cake	93	41	90
cooked, moist heat, 3 oz	87	14	85
raw, 1 crab	18	2	16
dungeness, raw, 1 crab	140	14	97
queen, raw, 3 oz	76	9	47
Crab apple, 1 C slices	83	3	0
Crab soup, 1 C	76	14	10
Cracker, cheese, plain, 10 crackers, 1″	50	21	6
sandwich w/peanut butter, 1 sandwich	40	18	1
graham, 2 crackers	60	9	0

	CAL	FAT (Cal)	CHOL (mg)
melba toast, 1 piece	20	tr	0
rye wafer, whole grain, 2 wafers	55	9	0
saltine, 4 crackers	50	9	4
snack type, 1 round cracker	15	9	0
wheat, thin, 4 crackers	35	9	0
whole wheat wafers, 2 crackers	35	18	0
Cranberry, 1 C whole	46	2	0
1 C chopped	54	2	0
Cranberry bean, boiled, ½ C	120	4	0
canned, ½ C	108	3	0
raw, ½ C	328	11	0
Cranberry juice cocktail, bottled, 1 C	147	1	0
Cranberry-orange relish, canned, ½ C	246	1	0
Cranberry sauce, canned, sweetened, ½ C	209	2	0
Crayfish, cooked, moist heat, 3 oz	97	10	151
raw, 8 fish	24	3	37
3 oz	76	8	118
Cream, imitation product, coffee whitener, liquid, 1 T	20	14	0
coffee whitener, powdered, 1 T	11	6	0
dessert topping, powdered, 1 T	8	5	0
dessert topping, prepared with whole milk, 1 T	8	5	tr
dessert topping, pressurized, 1 T	11	8	0
dessert topping, semi-solid, 1 T	13	9	0
sour dressing, nonbutterfat, filled-cream product, 1 C	21	17	1

	CAL	FAT (Cal)	CHOL (mg)
Cream, sweet, half-and-half, 1 T	20	2	6
heavy, unwhipped, 1 T	50	50	21
heavy, whipped, ½ C	405	198	81
light, table, 1 T	30	21	10
light, unwhipped, 1 T	45	45	17
light, whipped, ½ C	175	175	66
medium (25% fat), 1 T	37	34	13
whipped topping, 1 T	10	9	2
Cream of asparagus soup, condensed, 1 can	210	89	12
prepared w/whole milk, 1 C	161	74	22
prepared w/water, 1 C	87	37	5
dehydrated, 1 packet	234	62	1
Cream of celery soup, condensed, 1 can	219	122	34
prepared w/whole milk, 1 C	165	87	32
prepared w/water, 1 C	90	50	15
dehydrated, 1 packet	62	15	1
Cream of chicken soup, condensed, 1 can	283	161	24
prepared w/whole milk, 1 C	191	103	27
prepared w/water, 1 C	116	66	10
dehydrated, 1 packet	80	36	2
Cream of mushroom soup, condensed, 1 can	313	208	3
prepared w/whole milk, 1 C	203	122	20
prepared w/water, 1 C	129	81	2
Cream of onion soup, condensed, 1 can	NK	115	37
prepared w/whole milk, 1 C	NK	84	32
prepared w/water, 1 C	NK	47	15
Cream of potato soup, condensed, 1 can	178	52	15
prepared w/whole milk, 1 C	148	58	22

	CAL	FAT (Cal)	CHOL (mg)
prepared w/water, 1 C	73	21	5
Cream of shrimp soup, condensed, 1 can	219	114	40
prepared w/whole milk, 1 C	165	84	35
prepared w/water, 1 C	90	47	17
Cream of tomato soup, dehydrated, 1 C prepared	82	17	1
Cream of vegetable soup, dehydrated, 1 packet	79	38	0
Cream of Wheat®, instant, prepared, 1 C	140	tr	0
quick, 1 C	140	tr	0
regular, 1 C	140	tr	0
Creme de menthe, ⅔ fl oz	67	0	0
Croaker, Atlantic, breaded & fried, 3 oz	188	97	71
raw, 3 oz	89	24	52
Croissant, 1	235	108	13
Crookneck squash, boiled, ½ C	18	3	0
canned, ½ C slices	14	1	0
frozen, ½ C slices	24	2	0
raw, ½ C slices	12	1	0
Cucumber, 1	39	4	0
½ C slices	7	1	0
Cumin seed, 1 t	7	.5	0
Cupu assu oil, 1 T	120	120	0
1 C	1927	1927	0
Curacao, ⅔ fl oz	54	0	0
Cured beef, thin sliced, 5 slices	37	7	9
Curry powder, 1 t	7	0	0
Curry sauce, dehydrated, 1 packet	151	74	tr
prepared w/whole millk, 1 C	270	132	35
Currants, European black, ½ C	36	2	0
red, ½ C	31	1	0
white, ½ C	31	1	0
Zante, dried, ½ C	204	2	0
Cusk, raw, 3 oz	74	5	35

	CAL	FAT (Cal)	CHOL (mg)
Custard, baked, 1 C	305	135	278
Custard apple, 3.5 oz	101	5	0
Cuttlefish, raw, 3 oz	67	5	95
Daikon radish, boiled, ½ C slices	13	2	0
dried, ½ C	157	4	0
raw, 1 radish	62	3	0
½ C slices	8	tr	0
Daiquiri, 3.5 fl oz	122	0	0
Dandelion greens, boiled, ½ C chopped	17	3	0
raw, ½ C chopped	13	2	0
Danish pastry, 1 oz	110	54	24
fruit pastry, 1 round piece	235	117	56
packaged ring, 1/12 ring	109	53	24
round pastry, 1	220	108	49
Date, dry, 10 fruits	228	3	0
dry, 1 C chopped	489	7	0
natural, 10 fruits	288	3	0
natural, 1 C chopped	489	7	0
Dill, dried, 1 t	3	tr	0
Dill seed, 1 t	9	tr	0
Dock, boiled, 3/5 oz	20	6	0
raw, ½ C chopped	15	4	0
Dolphinfish, raw, 3 oz	73	5	62
Doughnut, cake type, plain, 1	210	108	20
yeast leavened, glazed, 1	235	117	21
Drum fish, raw, 3 oz	101	38	54
Duck, roasted, flesh only, ½ duck	445	225	197
Duck fat, 1 T	115	115	13
1 C	1846	1846	13
Dutch brand loaf, 2 slices	136	91	27
Eel, cooked, dry heat, 3 oz	200	114	137
raw, 3 oz	156	89	107
Egg, chicken, dried, whole, 1 T	30	19	96
whole, stabilized, 1 T	31	20	101

	CAL	FAT (Cal)	CHOL (mg)
white, stabilized flakes, ½ lb	796	1	0
white, stabilized powder, ½ lb	402	tr	0
fried, 1	83	58	246
hard boiled, 1	79	50	274
omelet, 1	95	64	248
poached, 1	79	50	273
raw, 1	79	50	274
scrambled, 1	95	68	248
white, raw, 1	16	tr	0
yolk, dried, 1 T	27	22	117
raw, 1	63	50	274
raw, frozen, ½ lb	733	585	2951
raw, frozen, sweetened, ½ lb	733	520	2627
Egg, duck, 1	130	87	619
Egg, goose, 1	267	172	NK
Egg, quail, 1	14	9	76
Egg, turkey, 1	135	84	737
Egg substitute, liquid, ¼ C	3	19	1
powder, 0.7 oz	88	23	113
Egg noodle, cooked, 1 C	200	18	50
Eggnog, 1 C	342	161	149
Eggplant, boiled, ½ C cubes	13	1	0
raw, ½ C cubes	11	.5	0
Elderberry, 1 C	105	6	0
Enchilada, 1	235	144	19
Endive, raw, 1 head	86	9	0
½ C chopped	4	.5	0
Eppaw, raw, ½ C	75	8	0
Escarole, 1 C chopped	10	tr	0
Escarole soup, 1 C	27	16	2
Falafel, 1 patty	57	27	0
Fava bean, boiled, ½ C	93	3	0
canned, ½ C	91	3	0

	CAL	FAT (Cal)	CHOL (mg)
raw, ½ C	256	10	0
Fennel seed, 1 t	7	tr	0
Fenu seed, 1 t	13	3	0
Fig, canned in extra heavy syrup, 3 fruits	91	1	0
in heavy syrup, 3 fruits	75	1	0
in light syrup, 3 fruits	58	1	0
in water, 3 fruits,	42	1	0
dried, cooked, ½ C	140	6	0
uncooked, ½ C	254	10	0
uncooked, 5 fruits	239	10	0
raw, 1 medium	37	1	0
1 large	47	2	0
Filbert, 1 C chopped	725	648	0
1 oz	180	162	0
Fish, *see specific types of fish*			
Fish sandwich, large, 1	470	243	91
regular, w/cheese, 1	420	207	56
Fish sticks, frozen, 1 stick	76	31	31
Flatfish, cooked, dry heat, 3 oz	99	12	58
raw, 3 oz	78	9	41
Fondant, uncoated, 1 oz	105	0	0
Frankfurter, beef, 8 per package, 1	180	146	35
10 per package, 1	142	116	27
beef & pork, 8 per package, 1	183	150	29
10 per package, 1	144	118	22
chicken, 1	116	79	45
turkey, 1	102	72	48
French bean, boiled, ½ C	111	6	0
raw, ½ C	316	17	0
French toast, home recipe, 1 slice	155	63	112
French onion soup, dehydrated, 1 packet	21	4	0
Fruit cocktail, canned in extra heavy syrup, ½ C	115	1	0

	CAL	FAT (Cal)	CHOL (mg)
in extra light syrup, ½ C	55	1	0
in heavy syrup, ½ C	93	1	0
in light syrup, ½ C	72	1	0
in juice, ½ C	56	tr	0
in water, ½ C	40	.5	0
Fruit punch, canned, 6 fl oz	85	0	0
Fruit salad, canned in extra heavy syrup,			
½ C	114	1	0
in heavy syrup, ½ C	94	1	0
in juice, ½ C	62	tr	0
in light syrup, ½ C	73	1	0
in water, ½ C	37	1	0
tropical, canned in heavy syrup, ½ C	110	1	0
Fudge, chocolate, 1 oz	115	27	1
Fuki, boiled, 3.5 oz	8	tr	0
canned, 1 C	3	1	0
raw, 1 C	13	.5	0
Garden cress, boiled, ½ C	16	.5	0
raw, 1 sprig	tr	tr	0
½ C	8	1	0
Garlic, raw, 1 clove	4	tr	0
Garlic powder, 1 t	5	0	0
Gazpacho, 1 C	57	20	0
Gefilte fish, commercial, sweet recipe, 1 piece	35	7	12
Gelatin, dessert, ½ C	70	0	0
unflavored, 1 packet	25	tr	0
Gin, 80 proof, 1.5 fl oz	95	0	0
86 proof, 1.5 fl oz	105	0	0
90 proof, 1.5 fl oz	110	0	0
94 proof, 1.5 fl oz	124	0	0
100 proof, 1.5 fl oz	133	0	0
Gin rickey, 1 glass	150	0	0
Ginger, dried, 1 t ground	6	tr	0

	CAL	FAT (Cal)	CHOL (mg)
raw, ¼ C slices	17	2	0
Goose fat, 1 T	115	115	13
1 C	1846	1846	205
Gooseberry, canned in light syrup, ½ C	93	2	0
raw, 1 C	67	8	0
Gourd, dishcloth, boiled, ½ C slices	50	3	0
raw, 1 C slices	10	1	0
dried strips, 3 strips	49	1	0
white-flowered, boiled, ½ C cubes	11	tr	0
raw, ½ C cubes	8	tr	0
Grape, American type, 10 fruits	15	1	0
black Corinth, dried, ½ C	204	2	0
Emperor, 10 fruits	40	tr	0
European type, 10 fruits	36	3	0
Thompson seedless, raw, 10 fruits	35	tr	0
canned in heavy syrup, 1 C	187	tr	0
canned in water, 1 C	97	2	0
Tokay, 10 fruits	40	tr	0
Grape drink, canned, 6 fl oz	100	0	0
Grape juice, canned or bottled, 1 C	155	2	0
frozen concentrate, sweetened, diluted, 1 C	128	2	0
undiluted, 6 fl oz	386	6	0
Grapefruit, canned in juice, ½ C	46	1	0
in light syrup, ½ C	76	1	0
in water, ½ C	44	1	0
raw, California & Arizona, pink & red, ½ fruit	46	1	0
1 C sections	86	2	0
Florida, pink & red, ½ fruit	36	1	0
1 C sections	68	2	0

	CAL	FAT (Cal)	CHOL (mg)
California, white, ½ fruit	43	1	0
1 C sections	84	2	0
Florida, white, ½ fruit	38	1	0
1 C sections	75	2	0
Grapefruit juice, canned sweetened, 1 C	116	2	0
unsweetened, 1 C	93	2	0
frozen concentrate, diluted, 1 C	102	3	0
undiluted, 6 fl oz	302	9	0
raw, 1 C	96	2	0
Grapeseed oil, 1 T	120	120	0
1 C	1927	1927	0
Great northern bean, boiled, ½ C	104	5	0
canned, ½ C	150	5	0
raw, ½ C	302	9	0
Green bean, boiled, ½ C	22	1	0
canned, ½ C	13	.5	0
seasoned, ½ C	18	2	0
frozen, ½ C	18	1	0
raw, ½ C	17	.5	0
Green pea soup, condensed, 1 can	398	64	0
prepared w/whole milk, 1 C	239	63	18
prepared w/water, 1 C	164	26	0
dehydrated, 6 fl oz prepared	100	11	0
Green pepper, sweet, boiled, 1 pepper	13	2	0
½ C chopped	12	2	0
canned, ½ C halves	13	2	0
freeze-dried, ¼ C	5	.5	0
frozen, chopped, 3.5 oz	18	2	0
raw, 1 pepper	18	3	0
½ C chopped	12	2	0
Groundberry, ½ C	37	4	0
Grouper, cooked, dry heat, 3 oz	100	10	40
raw, 3 oz	78	8	31

	CAL	FAT (Cal)	CHOL (mg)
Guava, common, 1 fruit	45	5	0
strawberry, 1 fruit	4	.5	0
Guava sauce, cooked, ½ C	43	2	0
Gum drop, 1 oz	100	tr	0
Haddock, cooked, dry heat, 3 oz	95	7	63
smoked, 3 oz	99	7	65
raw, 3 oz	74	5	49
Halibut, Atlantic & Pacific, cooked,			
dry heat, 3 oz	119	22	35
raw, 3 oz	390	0	27
Greenland, raw, 3 oz	158	106	39
Ham, chopped, canned, 1 slice, ¹⁄₁₆″	50	36	10
not canned, 1 slice, ¹⁄₁₆″	48	33	11
minced, 1 slice, ¹⁄₁₆″	55	39	15
roasted, light cure, lean,			
2.4 oz	105	36	37
lean & fat, 3 oz	205	126	53
sliced, extra lean, 1 slice,			
¹⁄₁₆″	37	13	13
regular, 1 slice, ¹⁄₁₆″	52	27	16
Ham & cheese loaf or roll, 1 slice,			
³⁄₃₂″	73	52	16
Ham & cheese spread, 1 T	37	25	9
1 oz	69	47	17
Ham salad spread, 1 T	32	21	6
1 oz	61	40	10
Hamburger, 1	245	99	32
¼ lb patty, 1	445	189	71
Hard candy, 1 oz	110	0	0
Hazelnut, 1 C chopped	725	648	0
1 oz	180	162	0
Hazelnut oil, 1 T	120	120	0
1 C	1927	1927	0
Headcheese, 1 slice, ³⁄₃₂″	60	40	23
Herring, Atlantic, cooked,			
dry heat, 3 oz	172	90	65

	CAL	FAT (Cal)	CHOL (mg)
kippered, 1 fillet	87	45	33
pickled, 1 piece	39	24	2
raw, 3 oz	134	69	51
Pacific, raw, 3 oz	166	106	65
Hollandaise sauce w/butterfat, dehydrated, 1 packet	187	140	40
prepared w/water, 1 C	237	178	51
w/vegetable oil, dehydrated, 1 packet	93	21	tr
prepared w/whole milk & butter, 1 C	703	147	189
Hominy grits, instant, 1 packet	80	tr	0
quick, 1 C	145	tr	0
regular, 1 C	145	tr	0
Honey, 1 T	65	0	0
Honey loaf, 1 slice, 3/32"	36	11	10
Honey roll sausage, 1 slice, 1/8"	42	22	12
Honeydew melon, 1/10 fruit	46	1	0
1 C cubed	60	2	0
Horseradish-tree leafy tip, boiled, 1/2 C chopped	25	4	0
raw, 1/2 C chopped	6	1	0
Horseradish-tree pod, boiled, 1/2 C slices	21	1	0
raw, 1/2 C slices	19	1	0
Hubbard squash, baked, 1/2 C cubes	51	6	0
boiled, 1/2 C mashed	35	4	0
raw, 1/2 C cubes	23	3	0
Hummus, 1/2 C	210	98	0
Hyacinth bean, boiled, 1/2 C	22	1	0
raw, 1/2 C	19	1	0
Hyacinth bean seed, boiled, 1/2 C	114	5	0
raw, 1/2 C	362	16	0
Ice cream, French vanilla, soft, 1 C	377	203	153
vanilla, 10% fat, 1 C	269	129	59
vanilla, 16% fat, 1 C	349	213	88

	CAL	FAT (Cal)	CHOL (mg)
Ice milk, vanilla, hard, 1 C	184	51	18
vanilla, soft, 1 C	223	42	13
Irishmoss, raw, 3.5 oz	49	1	0
Italian snap bean, boiled, ½ C	22	1	0
canned, ½ C	13	.5	0
seasoned, ½ C	18	2	0
frozen, ½ C	18	1	0
raw, ½ C	17	.5	0
Italian sausage, raw, 5 per lb, 1 link	315	257	69
4 per lb, 1 link	391	319	86
cooked, 5 per lb, 1 link	216	155	52
4 per lb, 1 link	268	192	65
Jackfruit, 3.5 oz	94	3	0
Jalapeno pepper, canned, ½ C chopped	17	4	0
Jam, 1 T	55	tr	0
1 packet	40	tr	0
Java plum, 3 fruits	5	tr	0
Jelly, 1 T	50	tr	0
1 packet	40	tr	0
Jelly bean, 1 oz	105	tr	0
Jerusalem artichoke, raw, ½ C slices	57	tr	0
Jew's ear, dried, ½ C	36	.5	0
raw, ½ C slices	13	tr	0
Jujube, dried, 3.5 oz	287	10	0
raw, 3.5 oz	79	2	0
Jute, boiled, ½ C	16	1	0
raw, ½ C	5	.5	0
Kale, boiled, ½ C chopped	21	2	0
frozen, ½ C chopped	20	3	0
raw, ½ C chopped	17	2	0
Kanpyo, 3 strips	49	1	0
Kelp, raw, ⅗ oz	43	5	0
Kidney bean, California red, boiled, ½ C	109	1	0

	CAL	FAT (Cal)	CHOL (mg)
raw, ½ C	304	2	0
red, boiled, ½ C	112	4	0
canned, ½ C	108	4	0
raw, ½ C	310	9	0
royal red, boiled, ½ C	108	1	0
raw, ½ C	303	4	0
Kidney bean sprouts, boiled, 3.5 oz	33	5	0
raw, ½ C	27	4	0
Kielbasa, 1 oz	88	69	19
Kiwifruit, 1 large	55	4	0
1 medium	46	3	0
Knockwurst, 1 link	209	170	39
Kohlrabi, boiled, ½ C slices	24	1	0
raw, ½ C slices	19	.5	0
Kumquat, 1 fruit	12	tr	0
Lamb, chop, arm, lean, braised, 1.7 oz	135	63	59
arm, lean & fat, braised, 2.2 oz	220	135	77
loin, lean, broiled, 2.3 oz	140	54	60
loin, lean & fat, broiled, 2.8 oz	235	144	78
leg, lean, roasted, 2.6 oz	140	54	65
lean & fat, roasted, 3 oz	205	117	78
rib, lean, roasted, 2 oz	130	63	50
lean & fat, roasted, 3 oz	315	234	77
Lambsquarters, boiled, ½ C chopped	29	.5	0
raw, 3.5 oz	43	1	0
Lard, 1 T	115	115	12
1 C	1849	1849	195
Laver, raw, 3.5 oz	35	3	0
Lebanon bologna, beef, 1 slice ⅛"	49	27	16
Leek, boiled, 1 leek	38	2	0
¼ C chopped	8	.5	0
freeze-dried, 1 T	1	tr	0

	CAL	FAT (Cal)	CHOL (mg)
raw, 1 leek	76	3	0
¼ C chopped	16	1	0
Leek soup, dehydrated, 1 C prepared	65	17	2
Lemon, w/peel, 1 medium	22	4	0
1 wedge	5	1	0
w/o peel, 1 large	25	2	0
1 medium	17	2	0
Lemon juice, canned or bottled, 1 C	52	6	0
1 T	3	.5	0
frozen, single strength, 1 C	53	1	0
1 T	3	.5	0
raw, 1 C	60	0	0
1 T	4	0	0
Lemon peel, 1 t	2	tr	0
1 T	5	tr	0
Lemonade, frozen concentrate, diluted, 6 fl oz	80	tr	0
undiluted, 6 fl oz	425	tr	0
Lentil, boiled, ½ C	115	3	0
raw, ½ C	324	8	0
Lentil sprouts, raw, ½ C	40	2	0
stir-fried, ⅗ oz	101	4	0
Lentil w/ham soup, 1 C	140	25	7
Lettuce, butterhead, 2 leaves	2	tr	0
1 head	21	3	0
Bibb, 2 leaves	2	tr	0
1 head	21	3	0
Boston, 2 leaves	2	tr	0
cos, 1 leaf	2	tr	0
½ C shredded	4	.5	0
iceberg, 1 leaf	3	.5	0
1 head	70	9	0
looseleaf, 1 leaf	2	tr	0
½ C shredded	5	1	0
romaine, 1 leaf	2	tr	0
½ C shredded	4	.5	0
1 head	21	3	0

	CAL	FAT (Cal)	CHOL (mg)
Lima bean, boiled, ½ C	104	2	0
canned, ½ C	93	3	0
frozen, baby, ½ C	94	2	0
fordhook, boiled, ½ C	85	3	0
raw, ½ C	88	6	0
Lima bean seed, boiled, baby ½ C	115	3	0
large, ½ C	108	3	0
canned, large, ½ C	95	2	0
raw, baby, ½ C	338	8	0
large, ½ C	301	5	0
Lima bean flour, 1 C	343	13	0
Lime, 1 fruit	20	1	0
Lime juice, canned or bottled, 1 C	51	5	0
1 T	3	.5	0
raw, 1 C	66	2	0
1 T	4	tr	0
Limeade, frozen conentrate, diluted, 6 fl oz	75	tr	0
undiluted, 6 fl oz	410	tr	0
Lingcod, raw, 3 oz	72	8	44
Linseed oil, 1 T	120	120	0
1 C	1927	1927	0
Liver cheese, 1 slice	115	87	66
Liverwurst, 1 slice, ¼"	59	46	28
Lobster, northern, cooked, moist heat, 3 oz	83	5	61
1.5 lb lobster	142	8	104
raw, 3 oz	77	7	81
1.5 lb lobster	136	12	143
Loganberry, frozen, 1 C	80	4	0
Longans, dried, 3.5 oz	286	.5	0
raw, 1 fruit	2	0	0
Loquat, 1 fruit	5	tr	0
Lotus root, boiled, 10 slices, ¼"	59	.5	0
raw, 10 slices, ¼"	45	1	0
Luncheon meat, beef, loaved, 1 slice, ³⁄₃₂"	87	67	18

	CAL	FAT (Cal)	CHOL (mg)
beef, thin sliced, 5 slices	26	6	9
beef & pork, 1 slice, 3/32"	100	82	15
pork, canned, 1 slice, 1/16"	70	57	13
Luncheon sausage, 1 slice, 10 per package	60	43	15
Lupins, boiled, 1/2 C	98	22	0
raw, 1/2 C	334	79	0
Luxury loaf, 1 slice, 3/32"	40	12	10
Lychee, dried, 3.5 oz	227	11	0
raw, 1 fruit	6	.5	0
Macadamia nut, roasted in oil, 1 C	960	927	0
1 oz	205	198	0
Macaroni, cooked firm, 1 C	190	9	0
cooked tender, served cold, 1 C	115	tr	0
served hot, 1 C	155	1	0
Macaroni & cheese, canned, 1 C	230	90	24
home recipe, 1 C	430	198	44
Mace, 1 t	10	1	0
Mackerel, Atlantic, cooked, dry heat, 3 oz	223	136	64
raw, 3 oz	174	106	60
jack, canned, 1 C	296	108	150
raw, 3 oz	133	60	40
king, raw, 3 oz	89	15	45
Pacific, raw, 3 oz	133	60	40
Spanish, cooked, dry heat, 3 oz	134	48	62
raw, 3 oz	118	48	65
Mammy apple, 1 fruit	431	38	0
Mango, 1 fruit	135	5	0
1 C slices	108	4	0
Manhattan, 3.5 fl oz	150	0	0
Maple syrup, 2 T	122	0	0
Margarine, hard, 1 t	34	34	0
1 stick	815	815	0

	CAL	FAT (Cal)	CHOL (mg)
imitation, 40% fat, 1 t	17	17	0
1 C	801	801	0
liquid, 1 t	34	34	0
1 C	1637	1637	0
soft, 1 t	34	34	0
1 C	1626	1626	0
spread, 60% fat, 1 t	25	25	0
1 C	1236	1236	0
Marinara sauce, canned, 1 C	171	75	0
Marjoram, dried, 1 t	4	0	0
Marshmallow, 1 oz	90	0	0
Martini, 3.5 fl oz	140	0	0
Masa harina, 1 C	404	40	0
Mayonnaise, safflower and soybean, 1 T	99	99	NK
soybean, 1 T	99	99	8
imitation, milk cream, 1 T	15	15	6
soybean, 1 T	35	26	4
soybean, no cholesterol, 1 T	68	60	0
Meat extender, simulated meat, 1 C	275	23	0
Melon balls, frozen (cantaloupe & honeydew), 1 C	55	4	0
Milk, chocolate, whole milk, 1 C	208	76	30
lowfat 1% milk, 1 C	158	23	7
lowfat 2% milk, 1 C	179	45	17
condensed, sweetened, 1 fl oz	123	31	13
dry, buttermilk, ¼ C	116	17	21
whole, ¼ C	149	77	33
nonfat, ¼ C	109	2	6
instant, ¼ C	224	4	12
calcium reduced, ¼ C	400	2	4
evaporated, skim, 1 fl oz	25	1	1
whole, 1 fl oz	42	21	9
filled, 1 C	154	72	4
goat, 1 C	168	91	28
hot cocoa, whole milk, 1 C	218	81	33

	CAL	FAT (Cal)	CHOL (mg)
human, 1 C	171	97	34
imitation, 1 C	150	75	tr
Indian buffalo, 1 C	236	151	46
low-fat, 1%, 1 C	102	23	10
w/nonfat milk solids added, 1 C	104	21	10
protein fortified, 1 C	119	26	10
low-fat, 2%, 1 C	121	41	18
w/nonfat milk solids added, 1 C	125	42	18
protein fortified, 1 C	137	44	19
malted, natural flavor, whole milk, 1 C	236	90	37
chocolate, whole milk, 1 C	233	82	34
powder, 1 T	86	17	4
sheep, 1 C	264	154	NK
skim, 1 C	86	4	4
protein fortified, 1 C	100	6	5
w/nonfat milk solids added, 1 C	90	5	5
thick shake, chocolate, 1 container	356	73	32
vanilla, 1 container	350	85	37
whey, acid, dry, 1 T	10	tr	NK
fluid, 1 C	59	2	NK
sweet, dry, 1 T	26	1	tr
fluid, 1 C	66	8	5
whole, 3.3% fat, 1 C	150	73	33
3.7% fat, 1 C	157	80	35
Milkfish, raw, 3 oz	126	51	44
Minestrone, chunky, 1 C	127	25	5
condensed, 1 can	202	55	3
prepared w/water, 1 C	83	23	2
dehydrated, 1 C prepared	62	12	1
Miso, ½ C	284	75	0
Mixed fruit, canned in heavy syrup, ½ C	92	1	0

	CAL	FAT (Cal)	CHOL (mg)
dried, 11 oz package	712	13	0
frozen, sweetened, 1 C	245	4	0
Mixed nuts, dry roasted, 1 oz	170	135	0
roasted in oil, 1 oz	175	144	0
Mixed vegetables, canned, ½ C	39	2	0
frozen, 1 C	54	1	0
Molasses, cane, blackstrap, 2 T	85	0	0
Monkfish, raw, 3 oz	64	12	21
Mortadella, 1 slice	47	34	8
Moth bean, boiled, ½ C	103	4	0
raw, ½ C	337	14	0
Mother's loaf, 1 slice, 1/16"	59	42	9
Mountain yam, Hawaii, raw, ½ C cubes	46	.5	0
steamed, ½ C cubes	59	.5	0
Muffin, commercial mix, blueberry, 1	140	45	45
bran, 1	140	36	28
corn, 1	145	54	42
home recipe, blueberry, 1	135	45	19
bran, 1	125	54	24
corn, 1	145	45	23
Mulberry, 10 fruits	7	.5	0
1 C	61	5	0
Mullet, striped, cooked, dry heat, 3 oz	127	37	54
raw, 3 oz	99	29	42
Mung bean, boiled, ½ C	107	4	0
long rice, dehydrated, ½ C	246	.5	0
raw, ½ C	361	11	0
Mung bean sprout, boiled, ½ C	13	5	0
canned, ½ C	0	tr	0
raw, ½ C	16	1	0
stir-fried, ½ C	31	1	0
Mungo bean, boiled, ½ C	95	4	0
raw, ½ C	365	2	0
Mushroom, boiled, ½ C pieces	21	3	0

	CAL	FAT (Cal)	CHOL (mg)
canned, ½ C pieces	19	2	0
raw, ½ C pieces	9	1	0
Mushroom barley soup, condensed, 1 can	NK	49	0
prepared w/water, 1 C	NK	20	0
Mushroom gravy, 1 can	150	73	0
2 T	15	7	0
dehydrated, 1 C prepared	70	8	1
Mushroom sauce, dehydrated, 1 packet	99	24	0
prepared w/whole milk, 1 C	228	93	34
Mushroom soup, dehydrated, 1 packet	74	34	0
w/beef stock, condensed, 1 can	208	88	18
prepared w/water, 1 C	85	36	7
Mussel, blue, cooked, dry heat, 3 oz	147	34	48
raw, 3 oz	73	17	24
Mustard, dried, 1 t	9	.5	0
prepared, 1 t	5	tr	0
Mustard greens, boiled, ½ C chopped	11	2	0
frozen, ½ C chopped	14	2	0
raw, ½ C chopped	7	.5	0
Mustard spinach, boiled, ½ C chopped	14	2	0
raw, ½ C chopped	17	2	0
Mutton tallow, 1 T	115	115	13
1 C	1849	1849	209
Natto, ½ C	187	87	0
Navy bean, boiled, ½ C	129	5	0
canned, ½ C	148	5	0
raw, ½ C	348	12	0
Navy bean sprouts, boiled, 3.5 oz	78	7	0
raw, ½ C	70	6	0
Nectarine, 1 fruit	67	6	0

	CAL	FAT (Cal)	CHOL (mg)
1 C slices	68	6	0
New England brand sausage, 1 slice	37	16	11
New Zealand spinach, boiled, ½ C chopped	11	1	0
raw, ½ C chopped	4	.5	0
Nori, 3.5 oz	35	3	0
Nutmeg, ground 1 t	11	.5	0
Nutmeg butter, 1 T	120	120	0
1 C	1927	1927	0
Oat bran, 1 oz	110	18	0
Oatmeal or rolled oats, nonfortified, instant 1 C	145	18	0
quick, 1 C	145	18	0
regular, 1 C	145	18	0
fortified, instant, plain, 1 C	105	18	0
flavored, 1 C	160	18	0
Ocean perch, Atlantic, cooked, dry heat, 3 oz	103	16	46
raw, 3 oz	80	13	36
Octopus, common, raw, 3 oz	70	8	41
Oheloberry, 10 fruits	3	tr	0
1 C	39	3	0
Okra, boiled, ½ C slices	25	1	0
frozen, ½ C slices	34	3	0
raw, ½ C slices	19	.5	0
Olive, canned, green, 4 medium or 3 extra large	15	18	0
ripe, mission, pitted, 3 small or 2 large	15	18	0
Olive loaf, 1 slice, 3/32"	67	42	11
Olive oil, 1 C	1909	1909	0
1 T	119	119	0
Onion, boiled, ½ C chopped	29	2	0
canned, ½ C chopped	21	1	0
dehydrated, 1 T flakes	16	tr	0
1 t powder	8	0	0

	CAL	FAT (Cal)	CHOL (mg)
frozen, chopped, ½ C	30	1	0
whole, 3.5 oz	28	.5	0
raw, ½ C chopped	27	2	0
Onion gravy, dehydrated, 1 C prepared	80	7	1
Onion ring, frozen, 2 rings	81	48	0
Onion soup, condensed, 1 can	138	38	0
prepared w/water, 1 C	57	16	0
dehydrated, 1 packet	21	4	0
Orange, California navel, 1 fruit	65	1	0
California Valencia, 1 fruit	59	3	0
Florida, 1 fruit	69	3	0
Orange juice, canned, 1 C	104	3	0
frozen concentrate, diluted, 1 C	112	1	0
undiluted, 6 fl oz	339	4	0
raw, 1 C	111	5	0
Orange-grapefruit juice, canned, 1 C	107	2	0
Orange peel, 1 T	4	tr	0
Oregano, dried, 1 t	6	tr	0
Oxtail soup, dehydrated, 1 C prepared	62	20	2
Oyster, Eastern, breaded & fried, 6 medium	173	100	72
3 oz	167	96	69
canned, 3 oz	58	19	46
cooked, moist heat, 6 medium	58	19	46
3 oz	117	38	93
raw, 6 medium	58	19	46
1 C	170	55	136
Oyster stew, condensed, 1 can	144	84	33
prepared w/whole milk, 1 C	134	71	32
prepared w/water, 1 C	59	34	14
Pak-choi, boiled, ½ C shredded	10	1	0
raw, ½ C shredded	5	.5	0

	CAL	FAT (Cal)	CHOL (mg)
Palm kernel oil, 1 T	120	120	0
1 C	1927	1927	0
Palm oil, 1 T	120	120	0
1 C	1927	1927	0
Pancake, buckwheat, from mix, 1 pancake	55	18	20
plain, from home recipe, 1 pancake	60	18	16
from mix, 1 pancake,	60	18	16
Papaya, 1 fruit	117	4	0
Papaya nectar, 1 C	142	3	0
Paprika, 1 t	7	tr	0
Parsley, dried, 1 t	4	0	0
freeze-dried, ¼ C	4	.5	0
raw, ½ C chopped	10	1	0
10 sprigs	5	tr	0
Passion-fruit, purple, 1 fruit	18	1	0
Passion-fruit juice, purple, 1 C	126	1	0
yellow, 1 C	149	4	0
Pastrami, beef, 2 slices	198	149	53
Parsnips, boiled, ½ C slices	63	2	0
raw, ½ C slices	50	2	0
Pate, goose liver, smoked, canned, 1 T	60	51	20
1 oz	131	112	43
Pe-tsai, boiled, ½ C shredded	8	1	0
raw, ½ C shredded	6	1	0
Pea, edible pod, boiled, ½ C	34	2	0
frozen, ½ C	42	3	0
raw, ½ C	30	1	0
green, boiled, ½ C	67	2	0
canned, ½ C	59	3	0
seasoned, ½ C	57	3	0
frozen, 1 C	63	2	0
raw, ½ C	63	3	0
split, boiled, ½ C	116	3	0
raw, ½ C	334	2	0

	CAL	FAT (Cal)	CHOL (mg)
Pea sprouts, boiled, 3.5 oz	118	5	0
raw, ½ C	77	4	0
Peach, canned in extra heavy syrup, 1 C	251	1	0
in extra light syrup, 1 C	104	2	0
in heavy syrup, 1 C	190	2	0
in juice, 1 C	109	1	0
in light syrup, 1 C	136	1	0
in water, 1 C	58	1	0
dehydrated, cooked, ½ C	61	5	0
uncooked, ½ C	188	5	0
dried, cooked, sweetened, ½ C halves	139	3	0
cooked, unsweetened, ½ C halves	99	3	0
uncooked, 10 halves	311	9	0
frozen, sliced, sweetened, ½ C	118	1	0
raw, 1 fruit	37	1	0
1 C slices	73	1	0
spiced, canned in heavy syrup, 1 fruit	66	1	0
Peach nectar, canned, 1 C	134	.5	0
Peanut, boiled, ½ C	102	63	0
dry roasted, ½ C	428	326	0
oil roasted, ½ C	419	20	0
raw, ½ C	414	323	0
Peanut butter, chunk style, 2 T	188	144	0
smooth style, 2 T	188	144	0
Peanut flour, 1 C	371	84	0
defatted, 1 C	196	3	0
low fat, 1 C	257	118	0
Peanut oil, 1 T	119	119	0
1 C	1909	1909	0
Pear, canned in extra heavy syrup, 1 half	77	1	0
in extra light syrup, 1 half	36	1	0

	CAL	FAT (Cal)	CHOL (mg)
in heavy syrup, 1 half	58	1	0
in juice, 1 half	38	.5	0
in light syrup, 1 half	45	tr	0
in water, 1 half	22	tr	0
dried, cooked, sweetened, ½ C	196	4	0
cooked, unsweetened, ½ C	163	4	0
uncooked, 10 halves	459	10	0
raw, bartlett, 1 pear	100	9	0
bosc, 1 pear	85	9	0
d'anjou, 1 pear	120	9	0
Pear nectar, canned, 1 C	149	tr	0
Peas & carrots, canned ½ C	48	3	0
frozen, ½ C	38	3	0
Peas & onions, canned, ½ C	30	2	0
frozen, ½ C	40	2	0
Pecan, 1 C halves	720	657	0
1 oz	190	171	0
Pepeao, dried, ½ C	36	.5	0
raw, ½ C slices	13	tr	0
Pepper loaf, 1 slice, ³⁄₃₂″	42	181	13
Pepperpot soup, condensed, 1 can	251	101	24
prepared w/water, 1 C	103	42	10
Perch, cooked, dry heat, 3 oz	99	9	98
raw, 3 oz	77	7	76
Persimmon, Japanese, dried, 1 fruit	93	2	0
raw, 1 fruit	118	3	0
native, raw, 1 fruit	32	1	0
Pickle, dill, 1 pickle	5	tr	0
fresh pack, 2 slices	10	tr	0
sweet gherkin, 1 pickle	20	tr	0
Pickle & pimiento loaf, 1 slice, ³⁄₃₂″	74	54	10
Picnic loaf, 1 slice, ³⁄₃₂″	66	42	11
Pie, apple, ⅙ pie	405	162	0
blueberry, ⅙ pie	380	153	0
cherry, ⅙ pie	410	162	0

	CAL	FAT (Cal)	CHOL (mg)
creme, ⅙ pie	455	207	8
custard, ⅙ pie	330	153	169
fried apple, 1 pie	255	126	14
fried cherry, 1 pie	250	126	13
lemon meringue, ⅙ pie	355	126	143
peach, ⅙ pie	405	153	0
pecan, ⅙ pie	575	288	95
pumpkin, ⅙ pie	320	153	109
Piecrust, from home recipe, 1 pie shell	900	540	0
from mix, crust for 2-crust pie	1485	837	0
Pigeon pea, boiled, ½ C	86	9	0
raw, ½ C	105	11	0
Pigeon pea seed, boiled, ½ C	102	3	0
raw, ½ C	350	14	0
Pike, northern, cooked, dry heat, 3 oz	96	7	43
raw, 3 oz	75	5	33
walleye, raw, 3 oz	79	9	73
Pine nut, shelled, 1 oz	160	153	0
Pineapple, canned in extra heavy syrup, ½ C	109	1	0
1 slice	48	.5	0
in heavy syrup, ½ C	100	1	0
1 slice	45	.5	0
in juice, ½ C chunks or tidbits	75	1	0
1 slice	35	.5	0
in light syrup, ½ C	116	1	0
1 slice	30	.5	0
in water, ½ C tidbits	40	1	0
1 slice	19	.5	0
frozen chunks, sweetened, ½ C	104	1	0
raw, 1 C diced	77	6	0

	CAL	FAT (Cal)	CHOL (mg)
1 slice	42	3	0
Pineapple-grapefruit juice drink, 6 fl oz	90	tr	0
Pineapple juice, canned, 1 C	139	2	0
frozen concentrate, diluted, 1 C	129	1	0
undiluted, 6 fl oz	387	2	0
Pink beans, boiled, ½ C	125	4	0
raw, ½ C	361	11	0
Pinto bean, frozen, 3 oz	460	4	0
Pinto bean seed, boiled, ½ C	117	4	0
canned, ½ C	93	3	0
raw, ½ C	326	10	0
Pinto bean sprout, boiled, 3.5 oz	22	3	0
raw, 3.5 oz	62	8	0
Pinyon, shelled, 1 oz	160	153	0
Pistachio nut, dried, shelled, 1 oz	165	126	0
Pitanga, 1 fruit	2	tr	0
1 C	57	6	0
Pizza, cheese, 1 slice	290	81	56
Plantain, cooked, ½ C slices	89	1	0
raw, 1 fruit	218	6	0
½ C slices	91	2	0
Planter's punch, 3.5 fl oz	175	0	0
Plum, purple, canned in extra heavy syrup, 3 fruits	135	1	0
in heavy syrup, 3 fruits	119	1	0
in juice, 3 fruits	55	tr	0
in light syrup, 3 fruits	83	1	0
in water, 3 fruits	39	tr	0
raw, 1 fruit	36	4	0
1 C slices	91	9	0
Poi, ½ C	134	2	0
Pokeberry shoot, boiled, ½ C	16	3	0
raw, ½ C	18	3	0
Polish sausage, 1 oz	92	73	20

	CAL	FAT (Cal)	CHOL (mg)
Pollock, Atlantic, raw, 3 oz	78	7	60
Walleye, cooked, dry heat, 3 oz	96	9	82
raw, 3 oz	68	6	61
Pomegranate, 1 fruit	104	4	0
Pompano, Florida, cooked, dry heat, 3 oz	179	93	54
raw, 3 oz	140	72	43
Popcorn, air popped, 1 C	30	tr	0
popped in vegetable oil, 1 C	55	27	0
sugar syrup coated, 1 C	135	9	0
Poppy seed, 1 t	13	1	0
Poppy-seed oil, 1 T	120	120	0
1 C	1927	1927	0
Popsicle, 3 fl oz	70	0	0
Pork, chop, loin, lean, broiled, 2.5 oz	165	72	71
pan fried, 2.4 oz	180	99	72
loin, lean & fat, broiled, 3.1 oz	275	171	84
pan fried, 3.1 oz	335	243	92
leg, lean, roasted, 2.5 oz	160	72	68
lean & fat, roasted, 3 oz	250	162	79
rib, lean, roasted, 2.5 oz	175	90	56
lean & fat, roasted, 3 oz	270	180	69
shoulder cut, lean, 2.4 oz	165	72	76
lean & fat, 3 oz	295	198	93
Pork gravy, dehydrated, 1 C prepared	76	17	3
Pork sausage, cooked, 1 link	48	36	11
1 patty	100	76	22
raw, 1 link	118	103	19
1 patty	238	207	39
Potato, au gratin, home recipe, ½ C	160	83	29
baked, 1 potato	220	2	0
flesh only, 1 potato	145	1	0
boiled, 1 potato	116	1	0

	CAL	FAT (Cal)	CHOL (mg)
canned, ½ C	54	2	0
cottage fries, frozen, 10 strips	109	37	0
dehydrated flakes, ½ C	361	6	0
dehydrated granules, w/o milk, dry, ½ C	80	2	0
w/milk, dry, ½ C	358	10	2
French-fries, frozen, fried in animal & vegetable oil, 10 strips	158	75	9
fried in vegetable oil, 10 strips	158	75	0
heated, 10 strips	111	39	0
frozen, whole, 3.5 oz	65	1	0
hash brown, home recipe, ½ C	163	98	0
frozen, ½ C	170	81	0
w/butter sauce, 3.5 oz	178	79	23
mashed, w/whole milk, ½ C	81	6	2
w/whole milk & margarine, ½ C	111	40	2
mashed, from dehydrated flakes, ½ C	118	53	15
from dehydrated granules w/o milk, ½ C	137	59	18
from dehydrated granules w/milk, ½ C	83	21	2
microwaved, flesh only, 1 potato	156	1	0
O'Brien, home recipe, ½ C	79	11	7
pancake, home recipe, 1 pancake, 3 oz	495	113	93
puff, frozen, 1 puff	16	7	0
raw, 1 potato	88	1	0
½ C diced	59	1	0
scalloped, home recipe, ½ C	105	40	14
Potato chips, 10 chips	105	64	0

	CAL	FAT (cal)	CHOL (mg)
1 oz	148	90	0
made from dried potatoes, 1 oz	164	118	0
Potato flour, 1 C	628	13	0
Potato salad, ½ C	179	92	86
Potato skin, raw, 1 potato's	22	.5	0
baked	115	.5	0
boiled	27	tr	0
microwaved	77	.5	0
Potato sticks, 1 oz package	148	88	0
Poultry salad sandwich spread, 1 T	26	16	4
1 oz	57	34	9
Pountry seasoning, 1 t	6	2	0
Pout, ocean, raw, 3 oz	67	7	44
Preserves, 1 T	55	tr	0
1 packet	40	tr	0
Pretzel, Dutch, 1	65	9	0
stick, 2.25″, 10 sticks	10	tr	0
twisted, thin, 10 pretzels	240	18	0
Prickley pear, 1 fruit	42	5	0
Prune, canned in heavy syrup, 5 fruits	90	1	0
dehydrated, cooked, ½ C	158	3	0
uncooked, ½ C	224	4	0
dried, cooked, sweetened, ½ C	147	2	0
cooked, unsweetened, ½ C	113	2	0
uncooked, 10 fruits	201	4	0
Prune juice, 1 C	181	1	0
Pudding, chocolate, canned, 1 can	205	99	1
mix, w/whole milk, ½ C	150	36	15
instant, w/whole milk, ½ C	155	36	14
rice, mix, w/whole milk, ½ C	155	36	15
tapioca, canned, 1 can	160	45	tr

	CAL	FAT (Cal)	CHOL (mg)
mix, w/whole milk, ½ C	145	36	15
vanilla, canned, 1 can	220	90	1
mix, w/whole milk, ½ C	145	36	15
instant, w/whole milk, ½ C	150	36	15
Pummelo, 1 fruit	228	2	0
1 C sections	71	1	0
Pumpkin, boiled, ½ C mashed	24	1	0
canned, ½ C	41	3	0
raw, ½ C cubes	15	.5	0
Pumpkin flower, boiled, ½ C	10	.5	0
raw, 1 C	5	tr	0
Pumpkin leaves, boiled, ½ C	7	1	0
raw, ½ C		1	0
Pumpkin pie mix, canned, 1 C	282	3	0
Pumpkin pie spice, 1 t	7	tr	0
Pumpkin seed, dry, hulled, 1 oz	155	117	0
Purslane, boiled, ½ C	10	1	0
raw, ½ C	4	.5	0
Quiche Lorraine, ⅛ of 8″ pie	600	432	285
Quince, 1 fruit	53	1	0
Radish, red, raw, 10 radishes	7	2	0
½ C slices	10	3	0
white icicle, raw, 1 radish	14	1	0
Radish sprouts, raw, ½ C	8	4	0
Raisin, golden, seedless, 1 C packed	498	7	0
1 C not packed	437	6	0
seeded, 1 C packed	488	8	0
1 C not packed	428	7	0
seedless, 1 C packed	494	7	0
1 C not packed	434	6	0
Rapeseed oil, 1 T	120	120	0
1 C	1927	1927	0
Raspberry, canned in heavy syrup, ½ C	117	1	0

	CAL	FAT (Cal)	CHOL (mg)
frozen, sweetened, ½ C	128	2	0
raw, 1 C	61	7	0
1 pint	154	16	0
Red cabbage, boiled, ½ C shredded	16	1	0
raw, ½ C shredded	10	1	0
Red pepper, sweet, boiled, 1 pepper	13	2	0
½ C chopped	12	2	0
canned, ½ C halves	13	2	0
freeze-dried, ¼ C	5	.5	0
frozen, chopped, 3.5 oz	18	2	0
raw, 1 pepper	18	3	0
½ C chopped	12	2	0
Red pepper, ground, 1 t	9	tr	0
Refried beans, canned, ½ C	134	12	0
Relish, sweet, 1 T	20	tr	0
Rhubarb, frozen, sweetened, ½ C	139	.5	0
raw, ½ C diced	13	1	0
Rice, brown, cooked, 1 C	230	18	0
white, instant, cooked, 1 C	180	0	0
parboiled, cooked, 1 C	185	tr	0
raw, 1 C	685	1	0
regular, cooked, 1 C	225	tr	0
raw, 1 C	670	9	0
Rice bran oil, 1 T	120	120	0
1 C	1927	1927	0
Rice flour, 1 C	479	4	0
Rice polishings, ½ C	220	63	0
Roast beef sandwich, 1	345	117	55
Rockfish, Pacific, cooked, dry heat, 3 oz	103	15	38
raw, 3 oz	80	12	29
Roe, raw, 1 oz	39	16	105
Rose-apple, 3.5 oz	25	3	0
Roselle, 1 C	28	3	0
Rosemary leaves, 1 t	5	tr	0
ground, 1 t	3	tr	0
Roughy, orange, raw, 3 oz	107	54	17

	CAL	FAT (cal)	CHOL (mg)
Rum, 80 proof, 1.5 fl oz	95	0	0
86 proof, 1.5 fl oz	105	0	0
90 proof, 1.5 fl oz	110	0	0
94 proof, 1.5 fl oz	124	0	0
100 proof, 1.5 fl oz	133	0	0
Rutabaga, boiled, ½ C cubes	29	1	0
raw, ½ C cubes	25	1	0
Rye flour, dark, 1 C	419	30	0
light, 1 C	314	8	0
medium, 1 C	308	14	0
Sablefish, raw, 3 oz	166	117	42
smoked, 3 oz	218	154	55
Safflower oil, 1 T	120	120	0
1 C	1927	1927	0
Saffron, 1 t	3	tr	0
Sage, 1 t	4	tr	0
Salad dressing, commercial, blue			
cheese, 1 T	77	72	NK
French, 1 T	67	55	NK
home recipe, 1 T	88	88	0
low calorie, 1 T	22	8	1
Italian, 1 T	69	64	NK
low calorie, 1 T	16	14	1
mayonnaise type, 1 T	57	44	4
Russian, 1 T	76	70	NK
low calorie, 1 T	23	6	1
sesame seed, 1 T	68	62	0
thousand island, 1 T	59	50	NK
low calorie, 1 T	24	14	2
vinegar and oil, home recipe, 1 T	72	72	0
Salami, beef, smoked, 1 slice, ⅛"	60	43	15
beef, cooked, 1 slice, ⅛"	58	42	14
beef & pork, 1 slice, ⅛"	57	42	15
dry or hard, pork & beef, 1 slice, 1/16"	42	31	8

	CAL	FAT (Cal)	CHOL (mg)
turkey, 2 slices	111	70	46
Salmon, Atlantic, raw, 3 oz	121	49	47
chinook, smoked, 3 oz	99	33	20
raw, 3 oz	153	80	56
chum, canned, 3 oz	120	42	33
raw, 3 oz	102	29	63
coho, cooked, moist heat, 3 oz	157	58	42
raw, 3 oz	124	46	33
pink, raw, 3 oz	99	26	44
sockeye, canned, 3 oz	130	56	37
cooked, dry heat, 3 oz	183	84	74
raw, 3 oz	143	65	53
Salsify, boiled, ½ C slices	46	1	0
raw, ½ C slices	55	1	0
Salt, 1 t	0	0	0
Sandwich spread, 1 T	35	23	6
1 oz	67	44	11
Sapodilla, 1 fruit	140	17	0
Sapote, 1 fruit	301	12	0
Sardine, Atlantic, canned in oil, 1 can	192	95	131
Pacific, canned in tomato sauce, 1 can	658	399	255
Sauerkraut, canned, ½ C	22	2	0
Sausage, beef, smoked, 1	134	104	29
simulated meat, 1 link	64	41	0
1 patty	97	62	0
Savory, 1 T	5	0	0
Savoy cabbage, boiled, ½ C shredded	18	.5	0
raw, ½ C shredded	10	.5	0
Scallop, breaded & fried, 2 large	67	31	19
imitation, 3 oz	84	3	18
raw, 2 large or 5 small	26	2	10
3 oz	75	6	28
Scallop squash, boiled, ½ C slices	14	1	0

	CAL	FAT (Cal)	CHOL (mg)
raw, ½ C slices	12	1	0
Scotch broth, condensed, 1 can	195	57	12
prepared w/water, 1 C	80	24	5
Scotch kale, boiled, ½ C chopped	18	2	0
raw, ½ C chopped	14	2	0
Sea bass, cooked, dry heat, 3 oz	105	20	45
raw, 3 oz	82	15	35
Seatrout, raw, 3 oz	88	28	71
Sesame oil, 1 T	120	120	0
1 C	1927	1927	0
Sesame seed, 1 T	45	36	0
Sesbania flower, boiled, ½ C	11	tr	0
raw, 1 C	5	tr	0
Shallot, freeze-dried, 1 T	3	0	0
raw, 1 T chopped	7	tr	0
Shark, batter dipped & fried, 3 oz	194	106	50
raw, 3 oz	111	34	43
Sherbet, orange, 1 C	270	34	14
Shellie bean, canned, ½ C	37	2	0
Shenut, 1 T	120	120	0
1 C	1927	1927	0
Shitake mushrooms, cooked, 4	40	1	0
dried, 1	11	.5	0
Shortening, household, 1 T	113	113	0
1 C	1812	1812	0
Shrimp, breaded & fried, 3 oz	206	94	150
4 large	73	33	53
canned, 3 oz	102	15	147
cooked, moist heat, 3 oz	84	8	166
4 large	22	2	43
imitation, 3 oz	86	11	31
raw, 3 oz	90	13	130
4 large	30	4	43
Small white bean, boiled, ½ C	127	5	0
raw, ½ C	363	11	0
Smelt, rainbow, cooked, dry heat, 3 oz	106	24	76

	CAL	FAT (Cal)	CHOL (mg)
raw, 3 oz	83	19	60
Smoked link sausage, pork, 1 link	265	194	46
1 little link	62	46	11
pork & beef, 1 link	229	186	48
1 little link	54	44	11
pork & beef, flour & nonfat dry milk added, 1 link	182	131	59
1 little link	43	31	14
pork & beef, nonfat dry milk added, 1 link	213	169	44
1 little link	50	40	10
Snap bean, boiled, ½ C	22	1	0
canned, ½ C	13	.5	0
seasoned, ½ C	18	2	0
frozen	18	1	0
raw, ½ C	17	.5	0
Snapper, cooked, dry heat, 3 oz	109	13	40
raw, 3 oz	85	10	31
Soda, club, 12 fl oz	0	0	0
cola, 12 fl oz	160	0	0
diet cola, 12 fl oz	tr	0	0
ginger ale, 12 fl oz	125	0	0
diet ginger ale, 12 fl oz	tr	0	0
grape	180	0	0
diet grape, 12 fl oz	tr	0	0
lemon-lime, 12 fl oz	155	0	0
diet lemon-lime, 12 fl oz	tr	0	0
orange, 12 fl oz	180	0	0
diet orange, 12 fl oz	tr	0	0
pepper type, 12 fl oz	160	0	0
diet pepper type, 12 fl oz	tr	0	0
root beer, 12 fl oz	165	0	0
diet root beer, 12 fl oz	tr	0	0
Sour cream, imitation, 1 oz	59	50	0
Sour cream, 1 T	25	21	5
half-and-half, 1 T	20	15	6

	CAL	FAT (Cal)	CHOL (mg)
Sour cream sauce, dehydrated, 1 packet	180	99	28
prepared w/whole milk, 1 C	509	272	91
Soursop, 1 fruit	416	17	0
1 C pulp	150	6	0
Soy milk, 1 C	79	41	0
Soy sauce, shoyu, 1 T	9	tr	0
tamari, 1 T	11	tr	0
vegetable protein, 1 T	7	tr	0
Soybean, boiled, ½ C	149	69	0
dry roasted, ½ C	387	167	0
raw, ½ C	387	167	0
roasted, ½ C	405	197	0
Soybean, green, boiled, ½ C	127	52	0
raw, ½ C	188	78	0
Soybean flour, defatted, 1 C	450	11	0
fat free, 1 C	303	0	0
high fat, 1 C	334	95	0
low fat, 1 C	356	60	0
Soybean oil, 1 T	120	120	0
1 C	1927	1927	0
Soybean sprouts, boiled, ½ C	38	19	0
raw, ½ C	45	21	0
stir-fried, 3.5 oz	125	64	0
Spaghetti, cooked al dente, 1 C	190	9	0
cooked tender, 1 C	155	1	0
Spaghetti & meatballs in tomato sauce,			
canned, 1 C	260	90	23
home recipe, 1 C	330	108	89
Spaghetti in tomato sauce w/cheese,			
canned, 1 C	190	18	3
home recipe, 1 C	260	81	8
Spaghetti sauce, canned, ½ C	136	53	0
dehydrated, 1 packet	118	4	0
w/mushrooms, 1 packet	118	32	11

	CAL	FAT (Cal)	CHOL (mg)
Spaghetti squash, baked or boiled, ½ C	23	2	0
raw, ½ C cubes	17	3	0
Spanish peanut, oil roasted, ½ C	426	324	0
raw, ½ C	417	326	0
Spinach, boiled, ½ C	21	2	0
canned, ½ C	25	5	0
frozen, 3 oz	19	5	0
raw, ½ C chopped	6	1	0
10-oz package	46	7	0
Spinach souffle, ½ C	109	83	0
Spiny lobster, raw, 1 lobster	233	28	146
3 oz	95	12	60
Spirulina, dried, 3.5 oz	290	69	0
raw, 3.5 oz	26	4	0
Split pea soup w/ham, chunky, 1 C	184	35	7
condensed, 1 can	459	96	20
prepared w/water, 1 C	189	40	8
dehydrated, 6 fl oz prepared	100	11	2
Spring onion, raw, ½ C chopped	13	.5	0
Squash, summer, boiled, ½ C slices	18	3	0
raw, ½ C slices	13	1	0
winter, baked, ½ C cubes	39	6	0
raw, ½ C cubes	21	1	0
Squash seed, dry, hulled, 1 oz	155	117	0
Squid, fried, 3 oz	149	57	221
raw, 3 oz	78	11	198
Stockpot, condensed, 1 can	242	85	9
prepared w/water, 1 C	100	35	5
Strawberry, canned in heavy syrup, ½ C	117	3	0
frozen, sweetened, slices, ½ C	123	1	0
sweetened, whole, ½ C	100	2	0
unsweetened, ½ C	26	1	0
raw, 1 C	45	5	0
1 pint	97	11	0

	CAL	FAT (Cal)	CHOL (mg)
Stroganoff, dehydrated, 1 packet	161	39	12
prepared w/whole millk & water, 1 C	271	96	38
Stuffing, bread, from mix, dry type, 1 C	500	279	0
moist type, 1 C	420	234	67
Succotash, boiled, ½ C	111	7	0
canned, w/cream style corn, ½ C	102	6	0
w/corn, ½ C	81	6	0
frozen, ½ C	79	7	0
raw, 3.5 oz	99	9	0
Sucker, white, raw, 3 oz	79	18	35
Sugar, brown, 1 C	820	0	0
white, granulated, 1 C	770	0	0
1 T	45	0	0
1 packet	25	0	0
1 t	15	0	0
white, powdered, 1 C	385	0	0
Sugar apple, 1 fruit	146	4	0
Summer sausage, beef, 1 slice	77	61	17
beef & pork, 1 slice, ⅛"	80	62	16
Sunfish, pumpkinseed, raw, 3 oz	76	5	57
Sunflower seed, dry hulled, 1 oz	160	126	0
Sunflower seed flour, partly defatted, 1 C	339	31	0
Sunflower oil, 1 T	120	120	0
1 C	1927	1927	0
Surimi, raw, 3 oz	84	7	25
Swamp cabbage, boiled, ½ C chopped	10	1	0
raw, 1 C chopped	11	1	0
Sweet & sour sauce, dehydrated, 1 packet	220	.5	0
prepared w/water & vinegar, 1 C	294	1	0
Sweet potato, baked in skin, 1 potato	118	1	0

	CAL	FAT (Cal)	CHOL (mg)
½ C mashed	103	1	0
boiled, ½ C mashed	172	4	0
candied, 1 piece 2.5″ long	144	31	8
canned, ½ C mashed	129	3	0
in syrup, ½ C	53	1	0
vacuum pack, ½ C pieces	92	2	0
frozen, ½ C cubes	88	1	0
raw, 1 C cubes	144	4	0
Sweet potato leaves, raw, 1 C chopped	12	1	0
steamed, ½ C	11	1	0
Swiss chard, boiled, ½ C chopped	18	.5	0
raw, 1 leaf	9	1	0
½ C chopped	3	.5	0
Swordfish, cooked, dry heat, 3 oz	132	39	43
raw, 3 oz	103	31	33
Taco, 1	195	99	21
Tahini, 1 T	90	72	0
Tahitian taro, cooked, ½ C slices	30	4	0
raw, ½ C slices	25	.5	0
Tamarind, 1 fruit	5	tr	0
½ C pulp	144	3	0
Tangerine, canned in juice, ½ C	46	tr	0
canned in light syrup, ½ C	76	1	0
raw, 1 fruit	37	1	0
Tangerine juice, canned, sweetened, 1 C	125	5	0
frozen concentrate, sweetened, diluted, 1 C	110	2	0
undiluted, 6 fl oz	344	7	0
raw, 1 C	106	4	0
Tarragon, 1 t	5	tr	0
Taro, cooked, ½ C slices	94	.5	0
raw, ½ C slices	56	1	0
Taro chip, 10 chips	110	53	0

	CAL	FAT (Cal)	CHOL (mg)
Taro leaves, raw, ½ C	12	1	0
steamed, ½ C	18	3	0
Taro shoot, cooked, ½ C slices	10	.5	0
raw, ½ C slices	5	.5	0
Teaseed oil, 1 T	120	120	0
1 C	1927	1927	0
Tempeh, ½ C	165	57	0
Teriyaki sauce, 1 T	15	0	0
dehydrated, 1 packet	130	8	0
prepared w/water, 1 C	131	8	0
Thuringer, beef & pork, 1 slice, ⅛"	80	62	16
Thyme, 1 t	5	0	0
Tofu, dried frozen (koyadofu), 1 piece	82	5	0
fried, 1 piece	35	24	0
fuyu (salted & fermented), 1 block	13	8	0
okara, ½ C	47	9	0
raw, firm, ¼ block	118	64	0
regular, ¼ block	88	6	0
Tomato, green, 1	30	2	0
red, boiled, ½ C chopped	30	3	0
canned, stewed, ½ C	34	2	0
whole, ½ C	24	3	0
w/green chilies, ½ C	18	1	0
raw, 1	24	2	0
1 C chopped	35	4	0
stewed, 1 C	59	20	0
Tomato beef w/noodle soup, condensed, 1 can	341	94	9
prepared w/water, 1 C	140	39	5
Tomato bisque soup, condensed, 1 can	300	55	11
prepared w/whole milk, 1 C	198	59	22
prepared w/water, 1 C	123	23	4
Tomato juice, canned, ½ C	21	.5	0
Tomato paste, ½ C	110	11	0

	CAL	FAT (Cal)	CHOL (mg)
Tomato powder, 3.5 oz	302	4	0
Tomato puree, canned, ½ C	56	1	0
Tomato rice soup, condensed, 1 can	291	59	3
prepared w/water, 1 C	120	24	2
Tomato sauce, canned, ½ C	37	2	0
Spanish style, ½ C	40	3	0
w/herbs & cheese, ½ C	72	21	NK
w/mushrooms, ½ C	42	1	0
w/onions, ½ C	52	2	0
w/onions, green peppers, & celery, ½ C	50	1	0
w/tomato tidbits, ½ C	39	4	0
Tomato seed oil, 1 T	120	120	0
1 C	1927	1927	0
Tomato soup, condensed, 1 can	208	42	0
prepared w/whole milk, 1 C	160	54	17
prepared w/water, 1 C	86	17	0
dehydrated, 1 C prepared	82	17	1
Tomato vegetable soup, dehydrated, 1 C prepared	55	8	tr
Tortilla, 1	65	9	0
Tortilla flour, yellow corn, 1 oz	101	10	0
white corn, 1 oz	103	14	0
Tree fern, cooked, ½ C chopped	28	.5	0
Trout, raw, 3 oz	126	51	49
Rainbow, cooked, dry heat, 3 oz	129	33	62
raw, 3 oz	100	26	48
Tumeric, 1 t	7	tr	0
Tuna, bluefin, fresh, cooked, dry heat, 3 oz	157	48	42
raw, 3 oz	122	38	32
light, canned in oil, 3 oz	169	63	15
skipjack, fresh, raw, 3 oz	88	8	40
white, canned in oil, 3 oz	158	62	26
canned in water, 3 oz	116	19	35

	CAL	FAT (Cal)	CHOL (mg)
yellowfin, fresh, raw, 3 oz	92	7	38
Tuna salad, 1 C	375	171	80
3 oz	159	71	11
Turkey, roasted, dark meat, 1 slice	40	14	18
light meat, 1 slice	68	14	30
light & dark, 1 C diced	240	63	106
roasted, frozen, boneless, light & dark meats, cooked, 3 oz	130	45	45
Turkey breast meat, 1 slice	23	3	9
Turkey fat, 1 T	115	115	13
1 C	1846	1846	209
Turkey gravy, 1 can	152	56	6
2 T	15	6	.5
dehydrated, 1 C prepared	87	17	3
Turkey ham, 2 slices	75	27	32
Turkey loaf, 2 slices	45	9	17
Turkey noodle soup, condensed, 1 can	168	43	12
prepared w/water, 1 C	69	18	5
Turkey patty, breaded & fried, 2.25 oz	180	108	40
Turkey roll, light, 2 slices	83	37	25
light and dark, 2 slices	84	36	31
Turkey salad with imitation mayo, 1 C	345	145	117
Turkey soup, chunky, 1 C	136	40	9
Turkey vegetable soup, condensed, 1 can	179	66	3
prepared w/water, 1 C	74	27	2
Turnip, boiled, ½ C cubes	14	.5	0
frozen, 3.5 oz	23	2	0
raw, ½ C cubes	18	.5	0
Turnip green, boiled, ½ C chopped	15	1	0
canned, ½ C	17	3	0
frozen, boiled, ½ C	24	3	0
raw, ½ C chopped	7	1	0

	CAL	FAT (Cal)	CHOL (mg)
Turnip greens & turnips, frozen, 3.5 oz	17	1	0
Tea	tr	tr	0
Tom Collins, 10 fl oz	180	0	0
Ucuhuba butter, 1 T	120	120	0
1 C	1927	1927	0
Valencia peanut, oil roasted, ½ C	424	332	0
raw, ½ C	817	313	0
Vanilla, 1 T	45	0	0
Veal, cutlet, braised or broiled, 3 oz	185	72	109
rib, medium fat, roasted, 3 oz boned	230	126	109
Vegetable beef soup, dehydrated, 1 C prepared	53	10	1
Vegetable juice cocktail, ½ C	22	1	0
Vegetable soup, chunky, 1 C	122	33	0
Vegetable w/beef broth, condensed, 1 can	197	42	6
prepared w/water, 1 C	81	17	2
Vegetable w/beef soup, condensed, 1 can	192	41	12
prepared w/water, 1 C	79	17	0
Vegetarian vegetable soup, condensed, 1 can	176	42	0
prepared w/water, 1 C	72	17	0
Vienna sausage, 1 sausage	45	36	8
Vine spinach, raw, 3.5 oz	19	3	0
Vinegar, cider, 1 T	tr	0	0
Virginia peanut, oil roasted, ½ C	413	313	0
raw, ½ C	411	320	0
Vodka, 80 proof, 1.5 fl oz	95	0	0
86 proof, 1.5 fl oz	106	0	0
90 proof, 1.5 fl oz	110	0	0
94 proof, 1.5 fl oz	124	0	0
100 proof, 1.5 fl oz	133	0	0

	CAL	FAT (Cal)	CHOL (mg)
Vienna sausage, canned, beef & pork, 1	45	36	8
Waffle, from mix, 1 waffle	205	72	59
home recipe, 1 waffle	245	117	102
Wakame, raw, 3.5 oz	45	6	0
Walnut, black, 1 C chopped	760	219	0
1 oz	170	144	0
English or Persian, 1 C pieces	770	666	0
1 oz	180	162	0
Walnut oil, 1 T	120	120	0
1 C	1927	1927	0
Water chestnuts, canned, ½ C slices	35	.5	0
raw, ½ C slices	66	.5	0
Watercress, raw, ½ C chopped	2	tr	0
Watermelon, 1/16 fruit	152	19	0
1 C diced	50	6	0
Wax gourd, boiled, ½ C cubes	11	2	0
raw, 1 C cubes	17	2	0
Welsh onion, raw, 3.5 oz	34	.5	0
Wheat flour, all-purpose, 1 C sifted	420	9	0
1 T sifted	46	1	0
1 C unsifted	455	9	0
1 T unsifted	51	1	0
bread, 1 C sifted	420	1	0
cake or pastry, 1 C sifted	350	9	0
self-rising, 1 C sifted	440	9	0
whole wheat, 1 C stirred	400	18	0
Wheat germ oil, 1 T	120	120	0
1 C	1927	1927	0
Whelk, cooked, moist heat, 3 oz	233	6	110
raw, 3 oz	117	3	55
Whiskey, 80 proof, 1.5 fl oz	95	0	0
86 proof, 1.5 fl oz	105	0	0
90 proof, 1.5 fl oz	110	0	0
94 proof, 1.5 fl oz	124	0	0

	CAL	FAT (Cal)	CHOL (mg)
100 proof, 1.5 fl oz	133	0	0
Whiskey sour, 3.5 fl oz	138	0	0
White bean, boiled, ½ C	125	3	0
canned, ½ C	153	3	0
raw, ½ C	337	8	0
White fish, raw 3 oz	114	5	51
smoked, 3 oz	92	7	28
White pepper, ground, 1 t	9	tr	0
White sauce, dehydrated, 1 packet	230	119	tr
prepared w/whole milk, 1 C	241	121	34
Whiting, cooked, dry heat, 3 oz	98	13	71
raw, 3 oz	77	10	57
Wine, Champagne, 4 fl oz	84	0	0
dessert, 18.8%, 3.5 fl oz	140	0	0
muscatel, 3.5 fl oz	158	0	0
port, 3.5 fl oz	158	0	0
red, 3.5 fl oz	75	0	0
rose, 3.5 fl oz	72	0	0
sauterne, 3.5 fl oz	85	0	0
sherry, 2 oz	84	0	0
vermouth, dry, 3.5 fl oz	105	0	0
vermouth, sweet, 3.5 fl oz	167	0	0
white, 3.5 fl oz	80	0	0
Winged bean, boiled, ½ C	12	2	0
raw, 1 C slices	22	3	0
Winged bean leaves, raw, 3.5 oz	74	10	0
Winged bean seed, boiled, ½ C	126	45	0
raw, ½ C	372	134	0
Winged bean tuber, raw, 3.5 oz	159	8	0
Witloof chicory, raw, ½ C	7	.5	0
Wolffish, Atlantic, raw, 3 oz	82	18	39
Yam, baked or boiled, ½ C cubes	79	1	0
raw, ½ C cubes	89	1	0
Yam bean, boiled, 3.5 oz	46	.5	0
raw, ½ C slices	25	1	0

	CAL	FAT (Cal)	CHOL (mg)
Yard-long bean, boiled, 1 pod	7	tr	0
½ C slices	25	.5	0
raw, 1 pod	6	.5	0
Yard-long bean seed, boiled, ½ C	102	4	0
raw, ½ C	292	10	0
Yeast, baker's, 1 packet	20	tr	0
brewer's, 1 T	25	tr	0
Yellow bean, boiled, ½ C	126	9	0
raw, ½ C	338	23	0
Yellow snap bean, boiled, ½ C	22	1	0
canned, ½ C	13	.5	0
seasoned, ½ C	18	2	0
frozen, ½ C	18	1	0
raw, ½ C	17	.5	0
Yogurt, low-fat, w/nonfat milk solids, 8 oz	144	32	14
coffee, 8 oz	194	26	11
fruit, w/9 g of protein, 8 oz	225	23	10
w/10 g of protein, 8 oz	231	22	10
w/11 g of protein, 8 oz	239	29	12
vanilla, 8 oz	194	26	11
skim, w/nonfat milk solids, 8 oz	127	4	4
whole milk, 8 oz	139	66	29
Yokan, 1 slice, ¼"	36	tr	0
Zucchini, boiled, ½ C slices	14	.5	0
frozen, ½ C	19	1	0
Italian style, canned, ½ C	33	1	0
raw, ½ C slices	9	1	0
Zwieback, 1 piece	30	6	1

PACKAGED FOODS

	CAL	FAT (Cal)	CHOL (mg)
Accent®, ½ t	5	0	0
Armour®			
Bacon, lower salt, cooked,			
.3-oz slice	38	29	6
.2-oz slice	30	24	5
Beef Bologna, 1 oz	90	81	15
lower salt, 1 oz	90	81	15
Beef Franks, 1	140	108	20
Bologna, 1 oz	90	81	15
lower salt, 1 oz	90	72	15
Cheddar Cheese, 1 oz	110	81	30
lower salt, 1 oz	110	81	30
Colby Cheese, 1 oz	110	81	30
lower salt, 1 oz	110	81	30
Cooked Salami, lower salt,			
1 oz	80	63	20
Franks, 1	140	117	25
Ham, lower salt, 1-oz slice	35	13	14
Hot Dogs, 1	190	158	28
Monterey Jack Cheese, 1 oz	110	81	30
lower salt, 1 oz	110	81	30
Star Bacon, cooked, .3-oz			
slice	38	28	5
.2-oz slice	29	22	5
Star Beef Bologna, 1 oz	100	81	15
Star Bologna, 1 oz	100	81	15

	CAL	FAT (Cal)	CHOL (mg)
Star Cooked Salami, 1 oz	80	63	20
Star Speedy Cut Ham, 1-oz slice	44	23	15
Arnold® Branola Country Oat, 1 slice	90	18	0
Branola Original, 1 slice	70	9	<1
Brick Oven Whole Wheat, 1 slice	60	18	0
Country White, 1 slice	100	18	<2
Light Golden Wheat, 1 slice	40	0	0
Light Italian, 1 slice	40	0	0
Light Oatmeal, 1 slice	40	0	0
Whole Wheat, 1 slice	60	18	<1
Aunt Jemima® Pancakes, mix, 1.2 oz	120	9	0
prepared (w/2% milk), 3–4 pancakes	200	62	74
Baken-ets® Fried Pork Skins, 1 oz	160	90	25
Baker's® Angel Flake®, bagged, ⅓ C	120	72	0
Angel Flake®, canned, ⅓ C	110	81	0
German's® Sweet Chocolate, 1 oz	140	90	0
Premium Coconut Shred, ⅓ C	140	81	0
Semi-Sweet Chocolate, 1 oz	140	81	0
Semi-Sweet Real Chocolate Chips, ¼ C	200	108	0
Semi-Sweet Chocolate Flavored Chips, ¼ C	190	81	0
Unsweetened Chocolate, 1 oz	140	135	0

	CAL	FAT (Cal)	CHOL (mg)
Banquet® All White Meat Fried			
Chicken Platter	430	189	105
All White Meat Hot 'n Spicy			
Fried Chicken Platter	430	189	105
Beans & Frankfurters Dinner	510	225	34
Beef Extra Helping Dinner	865	549	120
Beef Pie	500	288	25
Beef Platter	460	297	70
Chicken Pie	540	315	35
Chopped Beef Dinner	420	279	76
Family Favorite Chicken &			
Dumplings	420	216	43
Macaroni & Cheese	415	180	28
Noodles & Chicken	340	135	45
Spaghetti & Meatballs	290	81	28
Fish Platter	445	198	92
Ham Platter	400	144	49
Lasagna Extra Helping			
Dinner	645	207	38
Meat Loaf Dinner	440	243	82
Salisbury Steak Dinner	495	306	76
Salisbury Steak Extra			
Helping Dinner	910	540	171
w/Mushroom Gravy	890	522	169
Tuna Pie	540	297	27
Turkey Extra Helping Dinner	750	369	63
Turkey Dinner	385	180	37
Turkey Pie	500	279	37
Western Dinner	630	360	87
Betty Crocker® Fruit Corners®			
Apple Fruit Roll-Ups®, 1 roll	50	<9	0
Apricot Fruit Roll-Ups®,			
1 roll	50	<9	0
Banana Fruit Roll-Ups®,			
1 roll	50	<9	0

	CAL	FAT (Cal)	CHOL (mg)
Cherry Fruit Bars®, 1 bar	90	18	0
Cherry Fruit Roll-Ups®, 1 roll	50	<9	0
Cherry Fruit Wrinkles®, 1 pouch	100	18	0
Fruit Punch Fruit Roll-Ups®, 1 roll	60	9	0
Grape Fruit Bars®, 1 bar	90	18	0
Grape Fruit Roll-Ups®, 1 roll	50	<9	0
Grape Fruit Wrinkles®, 1 pouch	100	18	0
Lemon Fruit Wrinkles®, 1 pouch	100	18	0
Orange Fruit Roll-Ups®, 1 roll	50	<9	0
Orange Fruit Wrinkles®, 1 pouch	100	18	0
Orange-Pineapple Fruit Bars®, 1 bar	90	18	0
Potato Buds, 1 serving of mix	70	0	0
prepared w/margarine & whole milk	130	54	2
Raspberry Fruit Roll-Ups®, 1 roll	50	<9	0
Strawberry Fruit Bars®, 1 bar	90	18	0
Strawberry Fruit Roll-Ups®, 1 roll	50	<9	0
Strawberry Fruit Wrinkles®, 1 pouch	100	18	0
Tropical Fruit Bars®, 1 bar	90	18	0
Watermelon Fruit Roll-Ups®, 1 roll	60	9	0
Watermelon Fruit Wrinkles®, 1 pouch	100	18	0

	CAL	FAT (Cal)	CHOL (mg)
Birds Eye® Asparagus Cuts, 3.3 oz	25	0	0
Asparagus Spears, 3.3 oz	25	0	0
Baby Brussels Sprouts w/ Cheese Sauce, 4.5 oz	110	54	5
Baby Lima Beans, 3.3 oz	130	0	0
Bavarian Style Green Beans & Spaetzle, 3.3 oz	110	54	10
Big Ears® Corn on the Cob, 1 ear	160	9	0
Broccoli, Carrots, & Pasta Twists, 3.3 oz	90	36	0
Broccoli & Cauliflower w/ Creamy Italian Cheese Sauce, 4.5 oz	90	54	15
Broccoli, Cauliflower & Carrots w/Cheese Sauce, 5 oz	100	45	5
Broccoli Cuts, 3.3 oz	25	0	0
Broccoli Spears, 3.3 oz	25	0	0
Broccoli w/Cheese Sauce, 5 oz	120	54	5
Broccoli w/Creamy Italian Cheese Sauce, 4.5 oz	90	54	15
Brussels Sprouts, 3.3 oz	35	0	0
Cauliflower, 3.3 oz	25	0	0
Cauliflower w/Cheese Sauce, 5 oz	110	54	5
Chinese Style Stir-Fry Vegetables, 3.3 oz	35	0	0
Chinese Style Vegetables, 3.3 oz	80	45	0
Chopped Broccoli, 3.3 oz	25	0	0
Chopped Spinach, 3.3 oz	20	0	0
Chow Mein Style Vegetables, 3.3 oz	90	36	0
Cooked Winter Squash, 4 oz	45	0	0
Corn, Green Beans & Pasta			

	CAL	FAT (Cal)	CHOL (mg)
Curls, 3.3 oz	110	45	0
Corn on the Cob, 1 ear	120	9	0
Creamed Spinach, 3 oz	60	36	0
Cut Green Beans, 3 oz	25	0	0
Deluxe Artichoke Hearts, 3 oz	30	0	0
Deluxe Baby Broccoli Spears, 3.3 oz	30	0	0
Deluxe Baby Carrots, Peas and Pearl Onions, 3.3 oz	50	0	0
Deluxe Broccoli Florets, 3.3 oz	25	0	0
Deluxe Tender Sweet Corn, 3.3. oz	80	9	0
Deluxe Tender Tiny Peas, 3.3 oz	60	0	0
Deluxe Whole Baby Carrots, 3.3 oz	40	0	0
Deluxe Whole Green Beans, 3 oz	25	0	0
Farm Fresh Broccoli, Baby Carrots & Water Chestnuts, 3.2 oz	35	0	0
Farm Fresh Broccoli, Cauliflower & Carrots, 3.2 oz	25	0	0
Farm Fresh Broccoli, Corn & Red Peppers, 3.2 oz	50	0	0
Farm Fresh Broccoli, Green Beans, Pearl Onions & Red Peppers, 3.2 oz	25	0	0
Farm Fresh Broccoli, Red Peppers, Bamboo Shoots & Straw Mushrooms, 3.2 oz	25	0	0

	CAL	FAT (Cal)	CHOL (mg)
Farm Fresh Brussels Sprouts, Cauliflower & Carrots, 3.2 oz	30	0	0
Farm Fresh Cauliflower, Baby Whole Carrots & Snow Pea Pods, 3.2 oz	30	0	0
French Cut Green Beans, 3 oz	25	0	0
French Green Beans w/ Toasted Almonds, 3 oz	50	18	0
French Style Rice Recipe, 3.3 oz	110	0	0
Fordhook Lima Beans, 3.3 oz	100	0	0
Green Peas, 3.3 oz	80	0	0
Green Peas & Pearl Onons, 3.3 oz	70	0	0
Green Peas & Potatoes w/ Cream Sauce, 2.6 oz	130	54	0
Green Peas w/Cream Sauce, 2.6 oz	120	54	0
Italian Green Beans, 3 oz	30	0	0
Italian Style Rice Recipe, 3.3 oz	120	9	0
Italian Style Vegetables, 3.3 oz	110	63	0
Japanese Style Stir-Fry Vegetables, 3.3 oz	30	0	0
Japanese Style Vegetables, 3.3 oz	100	54	0
Little Ears® Corn on the cob, 2 ears	130	9	0
Mandarin Style Vegetables, 3.3 oz	90	36	0
Mixed Fruit in Syrup, 5 oz	120	0	0
Mixed Vegetables, 3.3 oz	60	0	0

	CAL	FAT (Cal)	CHOL (mg)
Mixed Vegetables w/Onion Sauce, 2.6 oz	100	45	0
New England Style Vegetables, 3.3 oz	130	63	0
Pasta Primavera Style Vegetables, 3.3 oz	120	45	5
Peas & Pearl Onions w/ Cheese Sauce, 5 oz	140	45	5
Red Raspberries in Lite Syrup, 5 oz	100	9	0
Rice & Green Peas w/Mushrooms, 2.3 oz	110	0	0
San Francisco Style Vegetables, 3.3 oz	100	45	0
Small Onions w/Cream Sauce, 3 oz	110	54	0
Small Whole Onions, 4 oz	40	0	0
Spanish Style Rice Recipe, 3.3 oz	110	0	0
Strawberries, in Lite Syrup, 5 oz	90	0	0
Strawberries in Syrup, 5 oz	120	0	0
Sweet Corn, 3.3 oz	80	9	0
Whole Leaf Spinach, 3.3 oz	20	0	0
Whole Strawberries in Lite Syrup, 5 oz	80	0	0
Bisquick®, 2 oz	230	63	0
Budget Gourmet® Beef Stroganoff Slim Select	280	90	60
Cauliflower Side Dish	110	45	25
Cheddared Potatoes Side Dish	230	117	35
Cheddared Potatoes & Broccoli Side Dish	130	36	25

	CAL	FAT (Cal)	CHOL (mg)
Cheese Manicotti Entree	450	234	50
Cheese Ravioli Slim Select	260	63	45
Cheese Tortellini Side Dish	180	54	15
Chicken-au-Gratin Slim Select	260	99	70
Chicken & Egg Noodles Entree	450	234	130
Chicken Cacciatore Three Dish Dinner	300	117	60
Chicken Enchilada Slim Select	270	63	50
Chicken w/Fettucini Entree	400	189	100
Country Style Corn Side Dish	140	45	15
Fettucini Slim Select	290	90	25
French Recipe Chicken Slim Select	260	90	60
Glazed Apples Side Dish	110	27	10
Glazed Turkey Slim Select	270	45	50
Ham & Asparagus Slim Select	280	90	40
Italian Sausage Lasagna Entree	420	180	80
Italian Style Meatballs Entree	310	108	55
Lasagna w/Meat Sauce Slim Select	290	90	25
Linguini w/Scallops & Clams Slim Select	280	99	60
Linguini w/Shrimp Entree	330	135	75
Macaroni & Cheese Side Dish	210	72	25
Mandarin Chicken Slim Select	290	54	25
Nacho Potatoes Side Dish	180	90	30
New England Recipe Vegetables Side Dish	210	90	20
New Potatoes Side Dish	120	54	20

	CAL	FAT (Cal)	CHOL (mg)
Oriental Beef Slim Select	290	81	25
Oriental Rice & Vegetables Side Dish	210	90	20
Pasta Alfredo Side Dish	200	72	25
Pasta Shells & Beef Entree	340	126	35
Peas & Cauliflower Side Dish	170	63	20
Peas & Water Chestnuts Side Dish	120	27	5
Pepper Steak Entree	300	81	25
Rice Pilaf Side Dish	240	81	90
Scallops & Shrimp Three Dish Dinner	320	81	70
Seafood Newberg Entree	350	108	70
Sirloin of Beef Slim Select	290	108	25
Sirloin Enchilada Slim Select	290	135	35
Sirloin Salisbury Steak Slim Select	280	72	75
Sirloin Salisbury Steak Three Dish Dinner	410	198	105
Sirloin Tips Entree	310	162	40
Sirloin Tips Three Dish Dinner	310	99	65
Sliced Turkey Three Dish Dinner	290	81	45
Spinach Au Gratin Side Dish	120	45	40
Spring Vegetables Side Dish	90	27	20
Swedish Meatballs Entree	600	351	140
Sweet & Sour Chicken Entree	350	63	40
Sweet Corn Side Dish	190	54	15
Teriyaki Chicken Three Dish Dinner	360	108	55
Three Cheese Lasagna Entree	400	153	65
Three Cheese Potatoes Side Dish	230	99	30
Turkey A La King Entree	390	162	75

	CAL	FAT (Cal)	CHOL (mg)
Veal Parmigiana Three Dish Dinner	440	180	165
Yankee Pot Roast Three Dish Dinner	380	189	70
Ziti Side Dish	220	81	15
Buitoni® Lasagna, 2 oz	210	9	0
Linguini, 2 oz	210	9	0
Mostaccioli Rigati, 2 oz	210	9	0
Rigatoni, 2 oz	210	9	0
Spaghetti, 2 oz	210	9	0
Spaghetti Twists, 2 oz	210	9	0
Spinach Shells, 2 oz	210	9	0
Tricolor Rotelle, 2 oz	210	9	0
Vermicelli, 2 oz	210	9	0
Wagon Wheels, 2 oz	210	9	0
Ziti, 2 oz	210	9	0
Butter Buds® sprinkles, ½ t	4	0	0
Casino® Havarti	120	99	35
Mozzarella Cheese, 1 oz	90	63	25
Romano Cheese, 1 oz	100	63	30
Catalina® French Dressing, 1 T	70	54	0
Reduced Calorie Dressing, 1 T	16	0	0
Cheez Whiz® Hot Mexican Pasteurized Processed Cheese Spread, 1 oz	80	54	15
Mild Mexican Pasteurized Processed Cheese Spread, 1 oz	80	54	15
Pasteurized Processed Cheese Spread, 1 oz	80	54	20

	CAL	FAT (Cal)	CHOL (mg)
Pasteurized Processed Cheese Spread w/Jalapeno Peppers, 1 oz	80	54	15
Pasteurized Processed Pimento Cheese Spread, 1 oz	80	54	15
Cheetos® Crunchy, 1 oz	160	90	0
Puffed Balls, 1 oz	160	90	0
Chun King® Beef Pepper Oriental	309	27	10
Beef Teriyaki	379	18	12
Chicken Chow Mein	361	45	23
Chicken Egg Rolls	210	63	18
Chinese Pea Pods, 6 oz	NK	NK	1
Crunchy Walnut Chicken	305	45	11
Fried Rice w/Chicken	254	36	33
w/Pork	263	45	24
Hunan Pork	324	54	9
Imperial Chicken	294	9	8
Meat/Shrimp Egg Rolls	214	72	18
Restaurant Egg Rolls	202	63	24
Shrimp Egg Rolls	189	54	18
Sweet & Sour Pork	394	36	6
Szechuan Beef	331	18	16
Columbo® Lowfat Lite Yogurts			
Banana Strawberry, 8 oz	190	<9	5
Blueberry, 8 oz	190	<9	5
Peach, 8 oz	190	<9	5
Raspberry, 8 oz	190	<9	5
Strawberry, 8 oz	190	<9	5
Vanilla, 8 oz	190	<9	5
Comstock® Apple Filling & Topping, 3.5 oz	120	0	0
Blueberry Filling & Topping, 3.5 oz	110	0	0

	CAL	FAT (Cal)	CHOL (mg)
Lite Cherry Filling & Topping, 3.5 oz	75	0	0
Cool Whip® Extra Creamy Dairy Recipe Whipped Topping, 1 T	16	9	0
Non-Dairy Whipped Topping, 1 T	12	9	0
Country Time®			
Lemon-Lime Drink Mix, sweetened, 8 fl oz	80	0	0
Lemon-Lime Drink Mix, sugar free, 8 fl oz	4	0	0
Lemonade Drink Mix, sweetened, 8 fl oz	80	0	0
Lemonade Drink Mix, sugar free, 8 fl oz	4	0	0
Pink Lemonade Drink Mix, sweetened, 8 fl oz	80	0	0
Pink Lemonade Drink Mix, sugar free, 8 fl oz	4	0	0
Cracker Barrel® Cheese Food w/Real Bacon, 1 oz	90	63	20
Extra Sharp Cheddar Cheese Food, 1 oz	90	63	20
Port Wine Cheddar Cheese Food, 1 oz	90	63	20
Port Wine Cheddar w/ Almonds, cheese log, 1 oz	90	54	15
Sharp Cheddar Cheese Food, 1 oz	90	63	20
Sharp Cheddar w/Almonds, cheese ball, 1 oz	90	54	15
Sharp Cheddar w/Almonds, cheese log, 1 oz	90	54	15

	CAL	FAT (Cal)	CHOL (mg)
Smokey Cheddar w/ Almonds, cheese log, 1 oz	90	54	15
Cream of Farina®, 3 T	120	0	0
w/ ¼ C skim milk	142	22	1
w/ ¼ C whole milk	159	38	9
Creamette® Egg Noodles, 2 oz	210	9	0
Fettuccini, 2 oz	210	9	0
Lasagna, 2 oz	210	9	0
Linguini, 2 oz	210	9	0
Macaroni, 2 oz	210	9	0
Rainbow Rotini, 2 oz	210	9	0
Rotini, 2 oz	210	9	0
Shells, 2 oz	210	9	0
Spaghetti, 2 oz	210	9	0
Ziti, 2 oz	210	9	0
Crisco®, 1 T	110	110	0
Butter Flavor, 1 T	110	110	0
Corn oil, 1 T	120	120	0
Oil, 1 T	120	120	0
Crystal Light® Berry Blend Drink Mix, sugar free, 8 fl oz	4	0	0
Berry Fruit Tea Drink Mix, sugar free, 8 fl oz	4	0	0
Caribbean Cooler Drink Mix, sugar free, 8 fl oz	4	0	0
Citrus Blend Drink Mix, sugar free, 8 fl oz	4	0	0
Citrus Fruit Tea Drink Mix, sugar free, 8 fl oz	4	0	0
Fruit Punch Drink Mix, sugar free, 8 fl oz	4	0	0

	CAL	FAT (Cal)	CHOL (mg)
Grape Drink Mix, sugar free, 8 fl oz	4	0	0
Iced Tea Drink Mix, sugar free, 8 fl oz	4	0	0
Lemonade Drink Mix, sugar free, 8 fl oz	4	0	0
Lemon-Lime Drink Mix, sugar free, 8 fl oz	4	0	0
Natural Brew Fruit Tea Drink Mix, sugar free, 8 fl oz	4	0	0
Orange Drink Mix, sugar free, 8 fl oz	4	0	0
Paradise Punch Drink Mix, sugar free, 8 fl oz	4	0	0
Tropical Fruit Tea Drink Mix, sugar free, 8 fl oz	4	0	0
Cup-A-Soup® Beef Flavor Noodle, 6 fl oz	45	<9	0
Chicken Flavor Cup-A-Broth, 6 fl oz	20	<9	0
Country Style Virginia Pea, 6 fl oz	150	54	0
Country Style Chicken Flavor & Sweet Corn, 6 fl oz	130	54	0
Country Style Chicken Flavor Supreme, 6 fl oz	110	54	0
Country Style Harvest Vegetable, 6 fl oz	80	1	0
Country Style Shrimp Flavor Bisque, 6 fl oz	180	99	0
Green Pea, 6 fl oz	110	36	6
Lite Broccoli, 6 fl oz	50	9	0
Lite French Onion, 6 fl oz	30	9	0
Lite Garden Primavera, 6 fl oz	25	<9	0

	CAL	FAT (Cal)	CHOL (mg)
Lite Oriental, 6 fl oz	30	9	0
Lots-A-Noodles® Beef Flavor, 6 fl oz	110	9	0
Lots-A-Noodles® Chicken Flavor, 6 fl oz	120	9	0
Lots-A-Noodles® Garden Vegetable, 6 fl oz	130	9	0
Onion, 6 fl oz	25	9	0
Ring Noodle Chicken Flavor, 6 fl oz	60	9	0
Spring Vegetable, 6 fl oz	40	<9	0
Tomato, 6 fl oz	100	9	0
Trim - 10 Calorie Beef Flavor, 6 fl oz	10	<9	0
Trim - 10 Calorie Beefy Tomato, 6 fl oz	10	<9	0
Trim - 10 Calorie Chicken Flavor, 6 fl oz	10	<9	0
Trim - 10 Calorie French Onion, 6 fl oz	10	<9	0
Trim - 10 Calorie Herb Vegetable, 6 fl oz	10	<9	0
D-Zerta® Low Calorie Gelatin, all flavors, ½ C	8	0	0
Butterscotch Reduced Calorie Pudding	25	0	0
prepared w/skim milk, ½ C	68	2	2
Chocolate Reduced Calorie Pudding	20	0	0
prepared w/skim milk, ½ C	63	2	2
Reduced Calorie Whipped Topping Mix, 1 T	8	8	0

	CAL	FAT (Cal)	CHOL (mg)
Vanilla Reduced Calorie Pudding	25	0	0
prepared w/skim milk, ½ C	68	2	2
Del Monte® Stewed Tomato, ½ C	35	0	0
Tomato Sauce, 1 C	70	0	0
no salt, 1 C	70	0	0
w/onion, 1 C	100	9	0
Delta Gold® Potato Chips, 1 oz	160	99	0
Dip Style Potato Chips, 1 oz	160	99	0
Doritos® Cool Ranch™ Tortilla Chips, 1 oz	140	63	0
Nacho Cheese Flavor, 1 oz	140	63	0
Salsa Rio Flavor, 1 oz	140	63	0
Taco Flavor, 1 oz	140	63	0
Tortilla Chips, 1 oz	140	54	0
Dream Whip® Whipped Topping Mix, 1 T	6	0	0
prepared w/whole milk	10	0	0
Drifted Snow® flour, 1 C	400	9	0
Duncan Hines® Angel Food Cake Mix, ½ mix	140	0	0
prepared, ½ cake	140	0	0
Bakery style Blueberry Muffin, ¹⁄₁₂ mix	180	45	0
prepared, 1	190	54	23
Bran & Honey Nut Muffin, ¹⁄₁₂ mix	190	54	0
prepared, 1	200	63	23
Cinnamon Swirl Muffin, ¹⁄₁₂ mix	190	54	0

	CAL	FAT (Cal)	CHOL (mg)
prepared, 1	200	63	23
Cranberry Orange Nut Muffin, ¹⁄₁₂ mix	190	63	0
prepared, 1	200	72	23
Pecan Crunch Muffin, ¹⁄₁₂ mix	210	90	0
prepared, 1	220	99	23
Chocolate Chip Cookie Mix, ¹⁄₁₈ mix	130	45	0
prepared, 2 cookies	132	46	15
Chocolate Frosting, ¹⁄₁₂ container	160	63	tr
Dark Dutch Fudge Frosting, ¹⁄₁₂ container	160	63	tr
Fudge Brownie Mix, ¹⁄₁₆ mix	120	27	0
prepared, 1	160	72	34
Chewey Recipe, ¹⁄₁₆ mix	100	18	0
prepared	130	45	17
Fudge Butter Recipe, ¹⁄₁₂ mix	190	36	0
prepared w/margarine, ¹⁄₁₂ cake	270	177	822
Golden Butter Recipe, ¹⁄₁₂ mix	190	36	0
prepared w/margarine, ¹⁄₁₂ cake	270	177	822
Milk Chocolate Frosting, ¹⁄₁₂ container	160	63	tr
Tradition Dark Dutch Fudge Mix, ¹⁄₁₂ mix	190	45	0
prepared w/margarine, ¹⁄₁₂ cake	280	135	822
Devil's Food Mix, ¹⁄₁₂ mix	190	45	0
prepared w/margarine, ¹⁄₁₂ cake	280	135	822
Fudge Marble Mix, ¹⁄₁₂ mix	190	36	0
prepared w/margarine, ¹⁄₁₂ cake	270	99	822

	CAL	FAT (Cal)	CHOL (mg)
French Vanilla Mix, 1/12 mix	190	36	0
prepared Lite, 1/12 cake	270	86	580
prepared w/margarine, 1/12 cake	260	99	822
Lemon Supreme Mix, 1/12 mix	190	36	0
prepared Lite, 1/12 cake	270	86	580
prepared w/margarine, 1/12 cake	260	99	822
Pineapple Supreme Mix, 1/12 mix	190	36	0
prepared w/margarine, 1/12 cake	260	99	822
Spice Mix, 1/12 mix	190	36	0
prepared w/margarine, 1/12 cake	260	99	822
Strawberry Supreme Mix, 1/12 mix	190	36	0
prepared Lite, 1/12 cake	270	86	580
prepared w/margarine, 1/12 cake	260	99	822
Swiss Chocolate Mix, 1/12 mix	190	45	0
prepared w/margarine, 1/12 cake	280	135	822
Yellow Mix, 1/12 mix	190	36	0
prepared Lite, 1/12 cake	270	86	580
prepared w/margarine, 1/12 cake	260	99	822
White Mix, 1/12 mix	190	36	0
prepared w/margarine, 1/12 cake	250	90	822
Vanilla Frosting, 1/12 container	160	63	tr
Wild Blueberry Muffin, 1/12 mix	100	27	0
prepared, 1	110	30	23

	CAL	FAT (Cal)	CHOL (mg)
El Charrito® Beef Enchilada Dinner	620	279	45
Cheese Enchilada Dinner	570	216	30
Chicken Enchilada Dinner	510	153	50
Corn Tortillas, 2	95	9	0
Flour Tortillas, 2	170	36	0
4 Grande Beef Enchiladas	890	423	65
Grande B&B Burrito, 1	430	144	25
Grande Beef Enchilada Dinner	950	441	70
Grande Green Chili B&B Burrito, 1	410	126	20
Grande Jalapeno Burrito, 1	410	135	25
Grande Mexican Style Dinner	850	423	65
Grande Red Chili B&B Burrito, 1	410	135	25
Grande Satillo Dinner	820	306	45
Green Chili B&B Burrito, 1	370	144	20
Mexican Style Dinner	690	315	45
Queso Dinner	490	144	15
Red Chili B&B Burrito, 1	380	162	20
Red Hot B&B Burrito, 1	540	162	20
Red Hot Beef Burrito, 1	340	153	20
Satillo Dinner	570	216	30
6 Beef & Cheese Enchiladas	880	378	70
6 Beef Enchiladas	880	441	75
6 Cheese Enchiladas	780	270	45
3 Beef Enchiladas	560	279	55
3 Cheese Enchiladas	470	180	30
3 Chicken Enchiladas	440	117	60
2 Grande Beef Enchiladas & 2 Soft Cheese Tacos & Beans	800	315	45
Equal®, 1 Packet	4	0	0

	CAL	FAT (Cal)	CHOL (mg)
Familia® Crunchy, 1 oz	116	27	0
w/ ¼ C whole milk	155	47	9
100% Natural, 2 oz	206	36	0
w/ ⅔ C skim milk	263	39	3
w/ ⅔ C whole milk	311	89	23
Original, 2 oz	212	27	0
w/ ⅔ C skim milk	269	30	3
w/ ⅔ C whole milk	317	80	23
Frito-Lay's® Cheese Filled			
Crackers, 1.5 oz	210	90	5
Cheese Flavored Pop Corn,			
1 oz	150	81	0
Fudge Nut Brownie, 2 oz	240	81	5
Peanut Butter Bar, 1.75 oz	270	144	0
Peanut Butter Filled			
Crackers, 1.5 oz	210	90	0
Fritos® Bar-B-Q Corn Chips, 1 oz	150	81	0
Chili Cheese Flavored Corn			
Chips, 1 oz	160	99	0
Corn Chips, 1 oz	150	90	0
Crisp 'N Thin Corn Chips,			
1 oz	160	90	0
Dip Size Corn Chips, 1 oz	150	81	0
Funyuns® Onion Flavored Snacks,			
1 oz	140	54	0
Gatorade® Citrus Cooler, 8 fl oz	50	0	0
Fruit Punch, 8 fl oz	50	0	0
Lemon-Lime, 8 fl oz	50	0	0
Lemonade, 8 fl oz	50	0	0
Orange, 8 fl oz	50	0	0
General Foods® Cafe Amaretto,			
6 fl oz	50	18	0

	CAL	FAT (Cal)	CHOL (mg)
Cafe Amaretto, sugar free, 6 fl oz	35	27	0
Cafe Francais, 6 fl oz	50	27	0
Cafe Francais, sugar free, 6 fl oz	35	18	0
Cafe Irish Creme, 6 fl oz	60	27	0
Cafe Irish Creme, sugar free, 6 fl oz	30	18	0
Cafe Vienna, 6 fl oz	60	18	0
Cafe Vienna, sugar free, 6 fl oz	30	18	0
Double Dutch Chocolate coffee, 6 fl oz	50	18	0
Irish Mocha Mint coffee, 6 fl oz	50	18	0
Irish Mocha Mint coffee, sugar free, 6 fl oz	25	18	0
Orange Cappuccino, 6 fl oz	60	18	0
Orange Cappuccino, sugar free, 6 fl oz	30	18	0
Suisse Mocha coffee, 6 fl oz	50	18	0
Suisse Mocha coffee, sugar free, 6 fl oz	30	18	0
General Mills® BooBerry®, 1 oz	110	9	0
w/ ½ C skim milk	153	11	2
w/ ½ C whole milk	188	49	18
Bran Muffin Crisp®, 1 oz	130	9	0
w/ ½ C skim milk	173	11	2
w/ ½ C whole milk	208	49	18
Brown Sugar & Honey Body Buddies®, 1 oz	110	<9	0
w/ ½ C skim milk	153	9	2
w/ ½ C whole milk	188	48	18
Cheerios®, 1 oz	110	18	0
w/ ½ C skim milk	153	20	2
w/ ½ C whole milk	188	58	18

	CAL	FAT (Cal)	CHOL (mg)
Cinnamon Toast Crunch™,			
1 oz	120	27	0
w/ ½ C skim milk	163	29	2
w/ ½ C whole milk	198	67	18
Circus Fun®, 1 oz	110	9	0
w/ ½ C skim milk	153	11	2
w/ ½ C whole milk	188	49	18
Clusters®, 1 oz	100	27	0
w/ ½ C skim milk	143	29	2
w/ ½ C whole milk	178	67	18
Cocoa Puffs®, 1 oz	110	9	0
w/ ½ C skim milk	153	11	2
w/ ½ C whole milk	188	49	18
Count Chocula®, 1 oz	110	9	0
w/ ½ C skim milk	153	11	2
w/ ½ C whole milk	188	49	18
Country® Corn Flakes, 1 oz	110	<9	0
w/ ½ C skim milk	153	9	2
w/ ½ C whole milk	188	48	18
Crispy Wheats 'n Raisins®,			
1 oz	110	9	0
w/ ½ C skim milk	153	11	2
w/ ½ C whole milk	188	49	18
Fiber One®, 1 oz	60	9	0
w/ ½ C skim milk	103	11	2
w/ ½ C whole milk	138	49	18
FrankenBerry®, 1 oz	110	9	0
w/ ½ C skim milk	153	11	2
w/ ½ C whole milk	188	49	18
Golden Grahams®, 1 oz	110	9	0
w/ ½ C skim milk	153	11	2
w/ ½ C whole milk	188	49	18
Honey Buc*Wheat Crisp™,			
1 oz	110	<9	0
w/ ½ C skim milk	153	9	2
w/ ½ C whole milk	188	48	18
Honey Nut Cheerios®, 1 oz	110	9	0

	CAL	FAT (Cal)	CHOL (mg)
w/ ½ C skim milk	153	11	2
w/ ½ C whole milk	188	49	18
Ice Cream Cones® Chocolate Chip, 1 oz	110	18	0
w/ ½ C skim millk	153	20	2
w/ ½ C whole milk	188	58	18
Ice Cream Cones® Vanilla, 1 oz	110	18	0
w/ ½ C skim milk	153	20	2
w/ ½ C whole milk	188	58	18
Instant Total™ Oatmeal, 1 oz	90	18	0
w/ ½ C skim milk	133	20	2
w/ ½ C whole milk	168	68	18
Apple Cinnamon, 1.25 oz	130	18	0
w/ ½ C skim milk	173	20	2
w/ ½ C whole milk	208	58	18
Cinnamon Raisin Almond, 1.5 oz	150	36	0
w/ ½ C skim milk	193	38	2
w/ ½ C whole milk	228	76	18
Mixed Nut, 1.3 oz	140	36	0
w/ ½ C skim milk	183	38	2
w/ ½ C whole milk	218	76	18
Kaboom®, 1 oz	110	9	0
w/ ½ C skim milk	153	11	2
w/ ½ C whole milk	188	49	18
Kix®, 1 oz	110	<9	0
w/ ½ C skim milk	153	9	2
w/ ½ C whole milk	188	48	18
Lucky Charms®, 1 oz	110	9	0
w/ ½ C skim milk	153	11	2
w/ ½ C whole milk	188	49	18
Natural Fruit Flavor Body Buddies®, 1 oz	110	9	0
w/ ½ C skim milk	153	11	2
w/ ½ C whole milk	188	49	18
Oatmeal Raisin Crisp®, 1 oz	110	18	0

	CAL	FAT (Cal)	CHOL (mg)
w/ ½ C skim milk	153	20	2
w/ ½ C whole milk	188	58	18
Quick Total™ Oatmeal, 1 oz	90	18	0
w/ ½ C skim milk	133	20	2
w/ ½ C whole milk	168	58	18
Raisin Nut Bran®, 1 oz	110	27	0
w/ ½ C skim milk	153	29	2
w/ ½ C whole milk	188	67	18
Rocky Road®, 1 oz	120	18	0
w/ ½ C skim milk	163	20	2
w/ ½ C whole milk	198	58	18
S'mores Crunch®, 1 oz	120	18	0
w/ ½ C skim milk	163	20	2
w/ ½ C whole milk	198	58	18
Total®, 1 oz	110	9	0
w/ ½ C skim milk	153	11	2
w/ ½ C whole milk	188	49	18
Total® Corn Flakes®, 1 oz	110	9	0
w/ ½ C skim milk	153	11	2
w/ ½ C whole milk	188	49	18
Trix®, 1 oz	110	9	0
w/ ½ C skim milk	153	11	2
w/ ½ C whole milk	188	49	18
Wheat Hearts®, 1 oz	110	9	0
Wheaties®, 1 oz	110	9	0
w/ ½ C skim milk	153	11	2
w/ ½ C whole milk	188	49	18
Gold Medal® All-Purpose flour, 1 C	400	9	0
Better for Bread™ High Protein flour, 1 C	400	9	0
Self-Rising flour, 1 C	380	9	0
Unbleached flour, 1 C	400	9	0
Whole Wheat Blend flour, 1 C	370	18	0
Whole Wheat Flour, 1 C	390	18	0

	CAL	FAT (Cal)	CHOL (mg)
Golden Grain® Macaroni &			
Cheese, 1.81 oz	190	19	4
prepared as directed	310	135	9
Pasta, plain, 2 oz	203	6	0
Stuffing, Chicken Flavor			
Bread, 1 oz	106	11	.4
prepared as directed	180	81	5
Cornbread Rice, 1 oz	105	9	.3
prepared as directed	180	81	5
Herb Butter Wild Rice,			
1 oz	104	10	.3
prepared as directed	180	81	5
Wild Rice Bread, 1 oz	108	10	.4
prepared as directed	180	81	5
Golden Image® American Flavored			
Imitation Pasteurized Processed			
Cheese Food, 1 oz	90	54	5
Cheddar Cheese, mild,			
imitation, 1 oz	110	81	45
Colby, imitation, 1 oz	110	81	45
Good Seasons® Salad Dressing Mix			
Buttermilk Farm Style	4	0	0
prepared, 1 T	60	54	5
Blue Cheese & Herbs	4	0	0
prepared, 1 T	80	80	0
Cheese Garlic	4	0	0
prepared, 1 T	80	80	0
Cheese Italian	4	0	0
prepared, 1 T	80	80	0
Classic Herb	2	0	0
prepared, 1 T	80	80	0
Garlic & Herbs	4	0	0
prepared, 1 T	80	80	0
Italian	2	0	0
prepared, 1 T	80	80	0

	CAL	FAT (Cal)	CHOL (mg)
Lemon & Herbs	2	0	0
prepared, 1 T	80	80	0
Lite Italian	4	0	0
prepared, 1 T	25	25	0
Lite Zesty Italian	4	0	0
prepared, 1 T	25	25	0
Mild Italian	4	0	0
prepared, 1 T	90	80	0
No Oil Italian Salad Dressing Mix, 1 T	6	0	0
Zesty Italian	2	0	0
prepared, 1 T	80	80	0
Grapes Alive® Grape Conserve, 1 t	14	0	0
Grandma's® Candied Animal Cookies, 1 oz	140	54	0
Chocolate Chip Big Cookies, 2	370	153	5
Chocolate Sandwich Cookies, 1.8 oz	260	108	0
Fudge Chocolate Chip Big Cookies, 2	350	117	5
Glazed Gingerbread Soft Cookies, 1 oz	120	27	0
Oatmeal Apple Spice Big Cookies, 2	330	108	10
Old Time Molasses Big Cookies, 2	320	81	5
Peanut Butter Big Cookies, 2	410	270	10
Peanut Butter Sandwich Creme Cookies, 1.8 oz	260	117	0
Rich'n Chewey® Chocolate Chip Cookies, 1 oz	140	54	5
Soft Raisin Big Cookies, 2	320	90	10
Vanilla Sandwich Creme Cookies, 1.8 oz	260	108	5

	CAL	FAT (Cal)	CHOL (mg)
Green Giant® Asparagus, 50% less salt, canned, ½ C	20	0	0
Asparagus Cuts/Spears, canned, ½ C	20	0	0
Asparagus Pilaf Microwave Garden Gourmet, ½ C	110	18	15
Blackeyed Peas, dry, ½ C	90	9	0
Broccoli Spears, frozen, ½ C	12	0	0
Brussels Sprouts, frozen, ½ C	25	0	0
Butter Beans, canned, ½ C	80	0	0
Caliente Style Chili Beans, canned, ½ C	100	9	0
Cauliflower Cuts, frozen, ½ C	12	0	0
Corn, 50% less salt, canned, ½ C	70	0	0
Dark Red Kidney Beans, canned, ½ C	90	0	0
Early June Peas, canned, ½ C	50	0	0
Early June Peas, frozen, ½ C	50	19	0
Fettucine Primavera Microwave Garden Gourmet, ½ C	130	27	30
French Style Cut Green Beans, canned, ½ C	20	0	0
Garbanzo Beans, canned, ½ C	90	18	0
Great Northern Beans, dry, ½ C	80	9	0
Green Beans, 50% less salt, canned, ½ C	20	0	0
Green Beans, frozen, ½ C	14	0	0
Harvest Fresh® Broccoli Cuts, ½ C	12	0	0

	CAL	FAT (Cal)	CHOL (mg)
Harvest Fresh® Cut Broccoli, ½ C	18	0	0
Harvest Fresh® Cut Green Beans, ½ C	16	0	0
Harvest Fresh® Early June Peas, ½ C	60	0	0
Harvest Fresh® Lima Beans, ½ C	60	0	0
Harvest Fresh® Mixed Vegetables, ½ C	45	0	0
Harvest Fresh® Niblets® Corn, ½ C	80	9	0
Harvest Fresh® Spinach, ½ C	25	0	0
Harvest Fresh® Sweet Peas, ½ C	50	0	0
Harvest Fresh® White Shoepeg Corn, ½ C	90	9	0
Kitchen Cut Green Beans, canned, ½ C	20	0	0
Light Red Kidney Beans, canned, ½ C	90	0	0
Lima Beans, frozen, ½ C	100	0	0
Mexicorn® w/ Peppers, canned, ½ C	80	9	0
Mini Sweet Peas, canned, ½ C	60	0	0
Mixed Vegetables, frozen, ½ C	50	0	0
Mushrooms: Pieces, Stems, & Buttons, canned, ½ C	25	0	0
Nibblers® Corn-on-the-Cob, 6 Ear, frozen, 2 ears	150	9	0
Niblets® Corn, frozen, ½ C	80	9	0
Niblets® Corn-on-the-Cob, 4 ear, frozen, 1 ear	150	9	0
Niblets® Golden Vacuum			

	CAL	FAT (Cal)	CHOL (mg)
Pack Corn, canned, ½ C	80	0	0
Oriental Straw Mushrooms, canned, ½ C	12	0	0
Oriental Style Microwave Garden Gourmet, ½ C	100	0	0
Pasta Dijon Microwave Garden Gourmet, ½ C	150	45	35
Picante Style Pinto Beans, dry, ½ C	100	9	0
Pinto Beans, canned, ½ C	90	9	0
Red Beans, dry, ½ C	90	9	0
Rotini Cheddar Microwave Garden Gourmet, ½ C	140	27	20
Spinach, frozen, ½ C	25	0	0
Sherry Wild Rice Microwave Garden Gourmet, ½ C	100	9	10
Sweet Peas, canned, ½ C	50	0	0
Sweet Peas, 50% less salt, canned, ½ C	50	0	0
Sweet Peas, frozen, ½ C	50	0	0
Sweet Peas & Onions, canned, ½ C	50	0	0
Three Bean Salad, canned, ½ C	70	0	0
Valley Combinations™ Broccoli Carrot Fanfare, ½ C	20	0	0
Valley Combination™ Broccoli Cauliflower Supreme, ½ C	20	0	0
Valley Combination™ Cauliflower Green Bean Festival, ½ C	16	0	6
Valley Combination™ Corn Broccoli Bounty, ½ C	45	9	0

	CAL	FAT (Cal)	CHOL (mg)
Valley Combination™ Sweet Pea Cauliflower Medley, ½ C	30	0	0
White Shoepeg Corn, frozen, ½ C	70	9	0
White Shoepeg Corn Vacuum Pak, canned, ½ C	90	0	0
Whole Kernel Corn, canned, ½ C	80	0	0
H-O® Instant Oatmeal, 1 oz	110	18	0
w/ ¼ C skim milk	133	22	1
w/ ¼ C whole milk	149	38	9
Raisins & Spice, 1.5 oz	150	18	0
w/ ¼ C skim milk	172	22	1
w/ ¼ C whole milk	189	38	9
Maple & Brown Sugar, 1⅓ oz	150	18	0
w/ ¼ C skim milk	172	22	1
w/ ¼ C whole milk	189	38	9
Natural & Artificial Flavors, 1.5 oz	160	18	0
w/ ¼ C skim milk	182	22	1
w/ ¼ C whole milk	199	38	9
Sweet & Mellow, 1⅓ oz	150	18	0
w/ ¼ C skim milk	172	22	1
w/ ¼ C whole milk	189	38	9
Handi-Snacks® Cheese 'n Crackers, 1 pkg	130	81	15
Peanut Butter 'n Cheese Crackers, 1 pkg	190	117	0
Harvest Moon Brand® Pasteurized Process Cheese Product (loaf), 1 oz	50	18	10

	CAL	FAT (Cal)	CHOL (mg)
Pasteurized Process Cheese			
Product American			
Flavored, 1 oz	70	36	15
Hawaiian Punch® Lite Fruit Juicy			
Red, 6 fl oz	60	0	0
Passion Fruit, 6 fl oz	100	0	0
Very Berry, 6 fl oz	90	0	0
Heartland® Natural Cereal, 1 oz	130	36	0
w/ ½ C skim milk	173	38	2
w/ ½ C whole milk	208	76	18
Natural Cereal Coconut			
Variety, 1 oz	130	45	0
w/ ½ C skim milk	173	47	2
w/ ½ C whole milk	208	85	18
Natural Cereal Raisin			
Variety, 1 oz	130	36	0
w/ ½ C skim milk	173	38	2
w/ ½ C whole milk	208	76	18
Heinz® Deep Fries Crinkle Cuts,			
3 oz	150	54	0
Deep Fries French Fries, 3 oz	160	54	0
Deep Fries Shoestrings, 3 oz	200	90	0
Hershey's® Chocolate Flavored			
Syrup, 1 oz	80	9	0
Cocoa, 1 oz	120	36	1
Instant Mix, ¾ oz	80	9	0
Kisses®, 1.46 oz	220	117	7
Milk Chocolate Bar, 1.65 oz	250	126	12
Milk Chocolate Bar w/			
Almonds, 1.55 oz	250	135	12
Special Dark®, 1.45 oz	220	108	3
Unsweetened Baking			
Chocolate, 1 oz	190	144	4

	CAL	FAT (Cal)	CHOL (mg)
Hickory Farms® German Sausage, 1 oz	100	72	20
Swedish Sausage, 1 oz	100	72	20
Hi-C® Cherry, 6 fl oz	100	0	0
Citrus Cooler, 6 fl oz	100	0	0
Fruit Punch, 6 fl oz	100	0	0
Hula Punch, 6 fl oz	80	0	0
Orange, 6 fl oz	100	0	0
Wild Berry, 6 fl oz	90	0	0
Hidden Valley Ranch® Blue Cheese Dressing, 1 T	58	54	5
Creamy Herb Dressing, 1 T	58	54	5
Original Buttermilk, 1 T	58	21	4
Original Ranch Dressing, 1 T	80	72	10
w/Bacon, 1 T	80	72	5
Ranch Style Italian Dressing, 1 T	70	63	0
Reduced Calorie Dressing, 1 T	35	27	4
Thousand Island Dressing, 1 T	60	45	0
Home Pride® Wheat, 1 slice	70	9	<5
White, 1 slice	70	9	<5
Hormel® Beef Stroganoff	280	81	48
Beef Sukiyaki	320	72	45
Boneless Beef Ribs	450	198	90
Chicken Acapulco	388	108	55
Chili Con Carne Suprema	380	171	65
Glazed Breast of Chicken	210	27	75
Italian Style Lasagna	350	144	40
Lemon Fillet of Cod	400	171	145
Linguini	350	162	85
Oriental Pepper Steak	280	90	57

	CAL	FAT (Cal)	CHOL (mg)
Spaghettini	220	27	5
Sweet & Sour Chicken	290	36	60
Tender Beef Roast	260	72	65
Hungry Jack® Potato Buds, 1			
serving of mix	70	0	0
prepared w/margarine &			
whole milk	140	63	4
Jell-O® Americana® Golden Egg			
Custard Mix	90	9	65
prepared w/whole milk,			
½ C	160	45	80
Americana® Rice Pudding	100	0	0
prepared w/whole milk,			
½ C	170	36	15
Americana® Chocolate			
Tapioca Pudding	90	9	0
prepared w/whole milk,			
½ C	170	45	15
Americana® Vanilla Tapioca			
Pudding	90	0	0
prepared w/whole milk,			
½ C	160	36	15
Banana Cream Instant			
Pudding & Pie			
Filling	90	0	0
prepared w/whole milk,			
½ C	160	36	15
Banana Cream Pudding &			
Pie Filling	50	0	0
prepared w/whole milk for			
8″ pie, ⅙ pie excluding			
crust	100	27	10
Banana Cream Sugar Free			
Instant Pudding & Pie			
Filling	30	0	0

	CAL	FAT (Cal)	CHOL (mg)
prepared w/2% low-fat milk, ½ C	90	18	10
Butter Pecan Instant Pudding & Pie Filling	100	9	0
prepared w/whole milk, ½ C	170	45	15
Butterscotch Instant Pudding & Pie Filling	90	0	0
prepared w/whole milk, ½ C	160	36	15
Butterscotch Pudding & Pie filling	90	0	0
prepared w/whole milk, ½ C	170	36	15
Butterscotch Sugar Free Instant Pudding & Pie Filling	30	0	0
prepared w/2% low- fat milk, ½ C	90	18	10
Cheesecake	160	36	0
prepared w/whole milk, ⅛ C	280	117	30
Chocolate Fudge Instant Pudding & Pie Filling	100	9	0
prepared w/whole milk, ½ C	180	45	15
Chocolate Fudge Pudding & Pie Filling	90	0	0
prepared w/whole milk, ½ C	160	36	15
Chocolate Fudge Sugar Free Instant Pudding & Pie Filling	40	9	0
prepared w/2% low-fat milk, ½ C	100	27	10
Chocolate Instant Pudding & Pie Filling	100	0	0

	CAL	FAT (Cal)	CHOL (mg)
prepared w/whole milk, ½ C	180	36	15
Chocolate Mousse Pie	150	45	0
prepared w/whole milk, ⅛ pie	250	135	30
Chocolate Pudding & Pie Filling	90	0	0
prepared w/whole milk, ½ C	160	36	15
Chocolate Pudding Pops® Bar, 1	80	18	0
Chocolate Sugar Free Instant Pudding & Pie Filling	35	0	0
prepared w/2% low-fat milk, ½ C	100	27	10
Chocolate Sugar Free Pudding & Pie Filling	30	0	0
prepared w/2% low-fat milk, ½ C	90	27	10
Chocolate-Caramel Swirl Pudding Pops® Bar, 1	80	18	0
Chocolate-Covered Chocolate Pudding Pops® Bar, 1	130	63	0
Chocolate-Covered Vanilla Pudding Pops® Bar, 1	130	63	0
Chocolate-Vanilla Swirl Pudding Pops® Bar, 1	70	18	0
Chocolate w/Chocolate Chips Pudding Pops® Bar, 1	80	27	0
Coconut Cream Instant Pudding & Pie Filling	100	18	0
prepared w/whole milk, ½ C	180	54	15
Coconut Cream Pie	160	63	0
prepared w/whole milk, ⅛ pie	260	153	30

	CAL	FAT (Cal)	CHOL (mg)
Coconut Cream Pudding & Pie Filling	60	18	0
prepared w/whole milk for 8″ pie, ⅙ pie excluding crust	110	36	10
French Vanilla Instant Pudding & Pie Filling	90	0	0
prepared w/whole milk, ½ C	160	36	15
French Vanilla Pudding & Pie Filling	90	0	0
prepared w/whole milk, ½ C	170	36	15
Fruit Bars, frozen, all flavors, 1	45	0	0
Gelatin, all flavors, ½ C	80	0	0
Gelatin Pops® Bars, frozen, all flavors, 1	35	0	0
Lemon Instant Pudding & Pie Filling	90	0	0
prepared w/whole milk, ½ C	170	36	15
Lemon Pudding & Pie Filling	50	0	0
prepared w/whole milk for 9″ pie, ⅙ pie excluding crust	170	18	90
Milk Chocolate Instant Pudding & Pie Filling	100	9	0
prepared w/whole milk, ½ C	180	45	15
Milk Chocolate Pudding & Pie Filling	90	0	0
prepared w/whole milk, ½ C	160	36	15
Pineapple Cream Instant Pudding & Pie Filling	90	0	0

	CAL	FAT (Cal)	CHOL (mg)
prepared w/whole milk, ½ C	160	36	15
Pistachio Instant Pudding & Pie Filling	100	9	0
prepared w/whole milk, ½ C	170	45	15
Pistachio Sugar Free Instant Pudding & Pie Filling	35	9	0
prepared w/2% low-fat milk, ½ C	100	27	10
Rich & Luscious® Chocolate Mousse	110	36	0
prepared w/whole milk, ½ C	150	54	10
Rich & Luscious® Chocolate Fudge Mousse	110	36	0
prepared w/whole milk, ½ C	150	54	10
Sugar Free Gelatin, all flavors, ½ C	8	0	0
Vanilla Instant Pudding & Pie Filling	90	0	0
prepared w/whole milk, ½ C	170	36	15
Vanilla Pudding & Pie Filling	80	0	0
prepared w/whole milk, ½ C	160	36	15
Vanilla Pudding Pops® Bar, 1	70	18	0
Vanilla Sugar Free Instant Pudding & Pie Filling	30	0	0
prepared w/whole milk, ½ C	90	18	10
Vanilla Sugar Free Pudding & Pie Filling	20	0	0
prepared w/2% low-fat milk, ½ C	80	18	10

	CAL	FAT (Cal)	CHOL (mg)
Vanilla w/Chocolate Chips Pudding Pops® Bar, 1	80	27	0
Jif®, Creamy, 2 T	190	144	0
Crunchy, 2 T	190	144	0
Joan Of Arc® Blackeyed Peas, canned, dry, ½ C	90	9	0
Butter Beans, canned, dry, ½ C	80	0	0
Caliente Style Chili Beans, canned, dry, ½ C	100	9	0
Dark Red Kidney Beans, canned, dry, ½ C	90	0	0
Garbanzo Beans, canned, dry, ½ C	90	18	0
Great Northern Beans, canned, dry, ½ C	80	9	0
Light Red Kidney Beans, canned, dry, ½ C	90	0	0
Mashed Yams, canned, ½ C	90	0	0
Picante Style Pinto Beans, dry, ½ C	100	9	0
Pinto Beans, ½ C	90	9	0
Red Beans, dry, ½ C	90	9	0
Yams in Heavy Syrup, ½ C	120	0	0
Yams in Light Syrup, ½ C	110	0	0
Yams in Pineapple Orange Sauce, ½ C	190	0	0
Juice Bowl® Apple Medley, 6 fl oz	90	0	0
Cranberry Medley, 6 fl oz	110	0	0
Grape Medley, 6 fl oz	105	0	0
Grapefruit Medley, 6 fl oz	75	0	0
Orange Medley, 6 fl oz	100	0	0
Pineapple Medley, 6 fl oz	90	0	0
Prune Medley, 6 fl oz	135	0	0

	CAL	FAT (Cal)	CHOL (mg)
Kellogg's® All-Bran®, 1 oz	70	9	0
w/ ½ C skim milk	113	11	2
w/ ½ C whole milk	148	49	18
w/ Extra Fiber, 1 oz	50	9	0
w/ ½ C skim milk	93	11	2
w/ ½ C whole milk	128	49	18
Apple Jacks®, 1 oz	110	0	0
w/ ½ C skim milk	153	2	2
w/ ½ C whole milk	188	40	18
Apple Raisin Crisp®, 1.3 oz	130	0	0
w/ ½ C skim milk	173	2	2
w/ ½ C whole milk	208	40	18
Blueberry Pop Tarts®, 1	210	45	0
Bran Flakes®, 1 oz	90	0	0
w/ ½ C skim milk	133	2	2
w/ ½ C whole milk	168	40	18
Brown Sugar Cinnamon Pop Tarts®, 1	210	72	0
Cherry Pop Tarts®, 1	210	45	0
Cocoa Krispies®, 1 oz	110	0	0
w/ ½ C skim milk	153	2	2
w/ ½ C whole milk	188	40	18
Common Sense® Oat Bran, 1 oz	100	9	0
w/ ½ C skim milk	143	11	2
w/ ½ C whole milk	178	49	18
w/Raisins, 1.3 oz	120	9	0
w/ ½ C skim milk	163	11	2
w/ ½ C whole milk	198	49	18
Corn Flakes, 1 oz	100	0	0
w/ ½ C skim milk	143	2	2
w/ ½ C whole milk	178	40	18
Corn Pops, 1 oz	110	0	0
w/ ½ C skim milk	153	2	2
w/ ½ C whole milk	188	40	18
Cracklin Oat Bran®, 1 oz	110	36	0
w/ ½ C skim milk	153	38	2

	CAL	FAT (Cal)	CHOL (mg)
w/ ½ C whole milk	188	76	18
Crispix®, 1 oz	110	0	0
w/ ½ C skim milk	153	2	2
w/ ½ C whole milk	188	40	18
Frosted Blueberry Pop Tarts®, 1	200	45	0
Frosted Brown Sugar Cinnamon Pop Tarts®, 1	210	63	0
Frosted Cherry Pop Tarts®, 1	210	45	0
Frosted Chocolate Fudge Pop Tarts®, 1	200	36	0
Frosted Dutch Apple Pop Tarts®, 1	210	54	0
Frosted Flakes®, 1 oz	110	0	0
w/ ½ C skim milk	153	2	2
w/ ½ C whole milk	188	40	18
Frosted Krispies®, 1 oz	110	0	0
w/ ½ C skim milk	153	2	2
w/ ½ C whole milk	188	40	18
Frosted Mini-Wheats®, 1 oz	100	0	0
w/ ½ C skim milk	143	2	2
w/ ½ C whole milk	178	40	18
Frosted Raspberry Pop Tarts®, 1	210	54	0
Frosted Strawberry Pop Tarts®, 1	200	45	0
Fruit Loops®	110	0	0
w/ ½ C skim milk	153	2	2
w/ ½ C whole milk	188	40	18
Fruitful Bran®, 1.3 oz	110	0	0
w/ ½ C skim milk	153	2	2
w/ ½ C whole milk	188	40	18
Fruity Marshmallow Krispies®, 1.3 oz	150	0	0
w/ ½ C skim milk	193	2	2
w/ ½ C whole milk	228	40	18

	CAL	FAT (Cal)	CHOL (mg)
Just Right® w/Fiber Nuggets, 1 oz	100	9	0
w/ ½ C skim milk	143	11	2
w/ ½ C whole milk	178	49	18
w/Fruit & Nuts	140	9	0
w/ ½ C skim milk	183	11	2
w/ ½ C whole milk	218	49	18
Meuslix®, 1.45 oz	130	9	0
w/ ½ C skim milk	173	11	2
w/ ½ C whole milk	208	49	18
Nut & Honey Crunch®, 1 oz	110	0	0
w/ ½ C skim milk	153	2	2
w/ ½ C whole milk	188	40	18
Nutri-Grain® Biscuits, 1 oz	90	0	0
w/ ½ C skim milk	133	2	2
w/ ½ C whole milk	168	40	18
Wheat, 1 oz	100	0	0
w/ ½ C skim milk	143	2	2
w/ ½ C whole milk	178	40	18
Wheat & Raisins, 1 oz	140	0	0
w/ ½ C skim milk	183	2	2
w/ ½ C whole milk	218	40	18
Nutrific® Oatmeal Flakes, 1.5 oz	110	0	0
w/ ½ C skim milk	153	2	2
w/ ½ C whole milk	188	40	18
Pro Grain®, 1 oz	100	0	0
w/ ½ C skim milk	143	2	2
w/ ½ C whole milk	178	40	18
Product 19®, 1 oz	100	0	0
w/ ½ C skim milk	143	2	2
w/ ½ C whole milk	178	40	18
Raisin Bran, 1.4 oz	120	9	0
w/ ½ C skim milk	163	11	2
w/ ½ C whole milk	198	49	18
Rice Krispies®, 1 oz	110	0	0

	CAL	FAT (Cal)	CHOL (mg)
w/ ½ C skim milk	153	2	2
w/ ½ C whole milk	188	40	18
Strawberry Pop Tarts®, 1	200	36	0
Squares®, Blueberry, 1 oz	90	0	0
w/ ½ C skim milk	133	2	2
w/ ½ C whole milk	168	40	18
Raisin, 1 oz	90	0	0
w/ ½ C skim milk	133	2	2
w/ ½ C whole milk	168	40	18
Kit Kat® wafer, 1.625 oz	250	117	12
Knox® Unflavored Gelatine, 1 T	25	0	0
Kool-Aid® Black Cherry, unsweetened	2	0	0
prepared w/sugar, 8 fl oz	100	0	0
Cherry, sugar free, 8 fl oz	4	0	0
Cherry, sugar sweetened, 8 fl oz	80	0	0
Cherry, unsweetened	2	0	0
prepared w/sugar, 8 fl oz	100	0	0
Cherry Kooler, 8.25 fl oz	130	0	0
Grape, sugar free, 8 fl oz	4	0	0
Grape, sugar sweetened, 8 fl oz	80	0	0
Grape, unsweetened	2	0	0
prepared w/sugar, 8 fl oz	100	0	0
Grape Kooler, 8.25 fl oz	130	0	0
Lemon-Lime, unsweetened	2	0	0
prepared w/sugar, 8 fl oz	100	0	0
Lemonade, sugar free, 8 fl oz	4	0	0
Lemonade, sugar sweetened, 8 fl oz	80	0	0
Lemonade, unsweetened	2	0	0
prepared w/sugar, 8 fl oz	100	0	0
Mountain Berry Punch, sugar			

	CAL	FAT (Cal)	CHOL (mg)
free, 8 fl oz	4	0	0
Mountain Berry Punch, sugar sweetened, 8 fl oz	80	0	0
Mountain Berry Punch, unsweetened	2	0	0
prepared w/sugar, 8 fl oz	100	0	0
Mountain Berry Punch Kooler, 8.25 fl oz	120	0	0
Orange, sugar free, 8 fl oz	4	0	0
Orange, sugar sweetened, 8 fl oz	80	0	0
Orange, unsweetened	2	0	0
prepared w/sugar, 8 fl oz	100	0	0
Orange Kooler, 8.25 fl oz	130	0	0
Pink Lemonade, sugar sweetened, 8 fl oz	80	0	0
Pink Lemonade, unsweetened	2	0	0
prepared w/sugar, 8 fl oz	100	0	0
Rainbow Punch, sugar free, 8 fl oz	4	0	0
Rainbow Punch, sugar sweetened, 8 fl oz	80	0	0
Rainbow Punch, unsweetened	2	0	0
prepared w/sugar, 8 fl oz	100	0	0
Rainbow Punch Kooler, 8.25 fl oz	130	0	0
Raspberry, sugar free, 8 fl oz	4	0	0
Raspberry, sugar sweetened, 8 fl oz	80	0	0
Raspberry, unsweetened	2	0	0
prepared w/sugar, 8 fl oz	100	0	0
Strawberry, sugar free, 8 fl oz	4	0	0
Strawberry, sugar sweetened, 8 fl oz	80	0	0

	CAL	FAT (Cal)	CHOL (mg)
Strawberry, unsweetened	2	0	0
prepared w/sugar, 8 fl oz	100	0	0
Strawberry Falls Punch, sugar free, 8 fl oz	4	0	0
Strawberry Falls Punch, sugar sweetened, 8 fl oz	80	0	0
Strawberry Falls Punch, unsweetened	2	0	0
prepared w/sugar, 8 fl oz	100	0	0
Sunshine Punch, sugar free, 8 fl oz	4	0	0
Sunshine Punch, sugar sweetened, 8 fl oz	80	0	0
Sunshine Punch, unsweetened	2	0	0
prepared w/sugar, 8 fl oz	100	0	0
Tropical Punch, sugar free, 8 fl oz	4	0	0
Tropical Punch, sugar sweetened, 8 fl oz	80	0	0
Tropical Punch, unsweetened	2	0	0
prepared w/sugar, 8 fl oz	100	0	0
Tropical Punch Kooler, 8.25 fl oz	130	0	0
Krackel® chocolate bar, 1.65 oz	250	126	9
Kraft® American Pasteurized Processed Cheese Spread, 1 oz	80	54	20
American Singles Pasteurized Processed Cheese Food, colored, 1 oz	90	63	20
American Singles Pasteurized Processed Cheese Food, white, 1 oz	90	63	20
American Style Spaghetti Dinner, 1 C	310	72	0

	CAL	FAT (Cal)	CHOL (mg)
Apple Juice, 6 fl oz	80	0	0
Avocado (Guacamole) Dip, 2 T	50	36	0
Bacon & Buttermilk Dressing, 1 T	80	72	0
Bacon & Horseradish Dip, 2 T	60	45	0
Bacon & Horseradish Dip, Premium, 2 T	50	45	10
Bacon & Tomato Dressing, 1 T	70	63	0
Bacon & Tomato Reduced Calorie, 1 T	30	18	0
Barbecue Sauce 2 T	40	9	0
Blue, 1 oz	100	81	30
Blue Cheese Dip, Premium, 2 T	45	36	10
Brick, 1 oz	110	81	30
Butter Mints, 1	8	0	0
Buttermilk & Chives Creamy Dressing, 1 T	80	72	5
Buttermilk Creamy Dressing, 1 T	80	72	5
Buttermilk Creamy Reduced Calorie, 1 T	30	27	0
Butterscotch Topping, flavored, 1 T	60	9	0
Caramel, 1	35	9	0
Caramel Topping, 1 T	60	0	0
Caraway, 1 oz	100	72	30
Cheddar, 1 oz	110	72	30
Cheeze 'N Bacon® Singles Pasteurized Processed Cheese Food, 1 oz	90	63	20
Chocolate Caramel Topping, 1 T	60	0	0
Chocolate Fudgies, 1	35	9	0

	CAL	FAT (Cal)	CHOL (mg)
Chocolate Topping, 1 T	50	0	0
Chunky Blue Cheese Dressing, 1 T	70	54	0
Chunky Blue Cheese Reduced Calorie, 1 T	30	18	0
Clam Dip, 2 T	60	36	10
Clam Dip, Premium, 2 T	45	36	20
Colby, 1 oz	110	81	30
Coleslaw Dressing, 1 T	70	54	10
Cream Style Prepared Horseradish, 1 T	8	0	0
Creamy Bacon Reduced Calorie Dressing, 1 T	30	18	0
Creamy Cucumber Dip, Premium, 2 T	50	36	10
Creamy Cucumber Dressing, 1 T	70	70	0
Creamy Cucumber Reduced Calorie, 1 T	30	27	0
Creamy Garlic Dressing, 1 T	50	45	10
Creamy Italian Dressing, 1 T	60	54	0
Creamy Italian Reduced Calorie, 1 T	25	18	0
Creamy Onion & Chives Dressing, 1 T	70	63	0
Creamy Onion Dip, Premium, 2 T	45	36	10
Deluxe® American Cheese (loaf), pasteurized, processed, 1 oz	110	81	25
Deluxe® American Cheese (slices), pasteurized, processed, 1 oz	110	81	25
Deluxe® Pimento Cheese Slices, pasteurized, processed, 1 oz	100	72	25

	CAL	FAT (Cal)	CHOL (mg)
Deluxe® Swiss Cheese Slices, pasteurized, processed, 1 oz	90	63	25
Edam, 1 oz	90	63	20
Egg Noodle & Cheese Dinner, ¾ C	340	153	50
Egg Noodle & Chicken Dinner, ¾ C	240	81	35
French Dressing, 1 T	60	54	0
French Onion Dip, 2 T	60	36	0
French Onion Dip, Premium, 2 T	45	36	10
French Reduced Calorie Dressing, 1 T	25	18	0
Fruit Salad, ½ C	50	0	0
Funmallows® marshmallows, 1	25	0	0
Garlic Dip, 2 T	60	36	0
Garlic Flavored Barbecue Sauce, 2 T	40	0	0
Golden Caesar Dressing, 1 T	70	63	0
Gouda, 1 oz	110	81	30
Grape Jelly Reduced Calorie, 1 t	6	0	0
Grapefruit Juice, unsweetened, 6 oz	70	0	0
Grapefruit Sections, unsweetened, ½ C	50	0	0
Green Onion Dip, 2 T	60	36	0
Hickory Smoke Flavored Barbecue Sauce, 2 T	40	9	0
Hickory Smoke flavored Onion Bits Barbecue Sauce, 2 T	50	9	0
Horseradish, prepared, 1 T	4	0	0
Horseradish Mustard, 1 T	4	0	0

	CAL	FAT (Cal)	CHOL (mg)
Horseradish Sauce, 1 T	50	45	5
Hot Barbecue Sauce, 2 T	40	9	0
Hot Fudge Topping, 1 T	70	27	0
Hot Hickory Smoke Flavored BBQ Sauce, 2 T	40	9	0
Italian Reduced Calorie Dressing, 1 T	6	0	0
Italian Seasonings Barbecue Sauce, 2 T	45	9	0
Jalapeno Pasteurized Process Cheese Spread, 1 oz	80	54	20
Jalapeno Pepper Dip, 2 T	50	36	0
Jalapeno Pepper Dip, Premium, 2 T	60	45	15
Jalapeno Pepper Spread, 1 oz	70	45	15
Jalapeno Singles Pasteurized Processed Cheese Food, 1 oz	90	63	25
Jam (all varieties), 1 t	18	0	0
Jelly (all varieties), 1 t	16	0	0
Jet Puffed-Marshmallows, 1	25	0	0
Kansas City Style Barbecue Sauce, 2 T	45	9	0
Light Reduced Calorie Mayonnaise, 1 T	45	45	5
Macaroni & Cheese Deluxe Dinner, ¾ C	260	72	20
Macaroni & Cheese Dinner, ¾ C	290	117	5
Malted Milk, chocolate, instant, made with 1 C whole milk	240	81	25
Malted Milk, natural, instant, made with 1 C whole milk	240	90	25
Marshmallow Cream, 1 oz	90	0	0
Mayonnaise, 1 T	108	108	5

	CAL	FAT (Cal)	CHOL (mg)
Mesquite Smoke Barbecue Sauce, 2 T	45	9	0
Miniature Funmallows®, 10	18	0	0
Miniature Marshmallows, 10	18	0	0
Monterey Jack, 1 oz	110	81	30
Monterey Jack Singles Pasteurized Processed Cheese Food, 1 oz	90	63	25
Monterey Jack w/Jalapeno Peppers, 1 oz	110	81	30
Monterey Jack w/Peppers, mild, 1 oz	110	81	30
Mozzarella Cheese, part skim, 1 oz	80	45	15
Mozzarella String Cheese w/Jalapeno Pepper, 1 oz	80	45	20
Muenster, 1 oz	110	81	30
Mustard, prepared, pure, 1 T	4	0	0
Nacho Cheese Dip, Premium, 2 T	50	36	10
Neufchatel, 1 oz	80	63	25
Oil & Vinegar Dressing, 1 T	70	63	0
Oil-Free Italian Dressing, 1 T	4	0	0
Old English® American Cheese (loaf), sharp, pasteurized, processed, 1 oz	110	81	30
American Cheese (slices), sharp, pasteurized, processed, 1 oz	110	81	30
Sharp Pasteurized Processed Cheese Spread, 1 oz	90	63	20
Olives & Pimento Spread, 1 oz	60	45	15
Onion Bits Barbecue Sauce, 2 T	50	9	0

	CAL	FAT (Cal)	CHOL (mg)
Orange Juice, unsweetened, 6 fl oz	90	0	0
Orange-Grapefruit Juice, unsweetened, 6 fl oz	80	0	0
Orange-Pineapple Juice, unsweetened, 6 fl oz	80	0	0
Parmesan, 1 oz	110	63	20
Parmesan, grated, 1 oz	130	81	30
Pasteurized Processed Cheese Food w/Bacon, 1 oz	90	63	20
w/Garlic, 1 oz	90	7	20
Pasteurized Processed Cheese Spread	80	54	20
w/Bacon, 1 oz	80	63	20
w/Garlic, 1 oz	80	54	15
Party Mints, 1	8	0	0
Peanut Brittle, 1 oz	140	45	0
Pimento Singles Pasteurized Processed Cheese Food, 1 oz	90	63	20
Pimento Spread, 1 oz	70	45	15
Pineapple Spread, 1 oz	70	45	15
Pineapple Topping, 1 T	50	0	0
Preserves (all varieties), 1 t	16	0	0
Provolone, 1 oz	100	63	25
Rancher's Choice Creamy Dressing, 1 T	80	72	5
Rancher's Choice Reduced Calorie, 1 T	30	27	5
Real Cream Topping, ¼ C	25	18	10
Red Raspberry Topping, 1 T	50	0	0
Red Wine Vinegar & Oil Dressing, 1 T	50	36	0
Relish Spread, 1 oz	70	45	15
Romano Cheese, grated, 1 oz	130	81	30
Russian Dressing, 1 T	60	45	0

	CAL	FAT (Cal)	CHOL (mg)
Russian Reduced Calorie Dressing, 1 T	30	9	0
Sandwich Spread, 1 T	50	45	5
Scamorze Cheese, part skim, 1 oz	80	45	15
Sharp Singles Pasteurized Processed Cheese Food, 1 oz	100	72	25
Spaghetti with Meat Sauce Dinner, 1 C	360	126	15
Spiral Macaroni & Cheese Dinner, ¾ C	330	153	10
Spread®, cup, 1 T	50	50	0
Spread®, stick, 1 T	60	60	0
Strawberry Preserves, Reduced Calorie, 1 t	8	0	0
Strawberry Topping, 1 T	50	0	0
Swiss, 1 oz	110	72	25
Swiss, aged, 1 oz	110	72	25
Swiss Singles Pasteurized Processed Cheese Food, 1 oz	90	63	25
Taco Shredded Cheese, 1 oz	110	81	30
Tangy Italian Style Spaghetti Dinner, 1 C	310	72	45
Tartar Sauce, 1 T	70	70	5
Thick'n Spicy Barbecue Sauce, 2 T	50	9	0
Chunky, 2 T	50	9	0
Hickory Smoked, 2 T	50	9	0
Kansas City Style, 2 T	60	9	0
w/Honey, 2 T	60	9	0
Thousand Island & Bacon Dressing, 1 T	60	54	0
Thousand Island Dressing, 1 T	60	45	5

	CAL	FAT (Cal)	CHOL (mg)
Thousand Island Reduced Calorie, 1 T	30	18	5
Toffee, 1	30	9	0
Walnut Topping, 1 T	90	45	0
Whipped Topping, 1¼ C	35	27	0
Zesty Italian Dressing, 1 T	70	70	0
Kretschmer® Honey Crunch Wheat Germ, 1 oz	105	25	0
Wheat Bran, 1 oz	57	21	0
Wheat Germ, 1 oz	103	31	0
La Pina® flour, 1 C	400	9	0
LaChoy® Almond Chicken	290	108	33
Almond Chicken Egg Rolls, 2	450	189	30
Beef & Broccoli	290	63	54
Beef & Broccoli Egg Rolls, 2	380	117	41
Beef Teriyaki	280	63	48
Imperial Chicken Chow Mein	270	63	45
Pepper Steak	290	81	54
Shrimp w/Lobster Sauce	220	63	99
Spicy Chicken Oriental	290	45	27
Spicy Oriental Chicken Egg Rolls, 2	300	90	32
Sweet & Sour Chicken	280	36	33
Sweet & Sour Pork Egg Rolls, 2	430	135	41
Lay's® Bar-B-Q Flavored Potato Chips, 1 oz	150	81	0
Italian Cheese flavored Potato Chips, 1 oz	150	81	0
Jalapeno 'N Cheddar Flavored Potato Chips, 1 oz	150	81	0

	CAL	FAT (Cal)	CHOL (mg)
Potato Chips, 1 oz	150	90	0
Salt & Vinegar Flavored Potato Chips, 1 oz	150	81	0
Sour Cream & Onion Flavored Potato Chips, 1 oz	150	90	0
Unsalted Potato Chips, 1 oz	150	90	0
Lay's® Crunch Tators™ Amazin' Cajun™ Flavor Potato Chips, 1 oz	140	63	0
Hoppin' Jalapeno™ Flavor, 1 oz	140	63	0
Mighty Mesquite BBQ Flavor, 1 oz	140	63	0
Potato Chips	140	63	0
Libby's® Pumpkin, solid pack, 1 C	80	9	0
Pumpkin Pie Mix, 10 oz	230	0	tr
Light N' Lively® American flavor Pasteurized Processed Cheese Product, singles, 1 oz	70	36	15
Sharp Cheddar Flavored Pasteurized Processed Cheese Product, singles, 1 oz	70	36	15
Swiss flavored Pasteurized Processed Cheese Product, singles, 1 oz	70	36	15
Lunch Wagon® Pizza Topping, 1 oz	80	54	0
Sandwich Slices, 1 oz	80	54	5
Maltex®, 1 oz	105	<9	0
Maypo® Oat Cereal-Maple Flavor, 1 oz	105	9	0
Oatmeal-Maple Flavor, ¼ C	101	9	0

	CAL	FAT (Cal)	CHOL (mg)
Minute® Rice, prepared, plain, ⅔ C	120	0	0
Drumstick Mix	120	0	0
prepared w/butter, ½ C	150	36	10
Fried Rice Mix	120	0	0
prepared w/oil, ½ C	160	45	0
Long Grain & Wild Rice Mix	120	0	0
prepared w/butter, ½ C	150	36	10
Rib Roast Mix	120	0	0
prepared w/butter, ½ C	150	36	10
Miracle® Whipped Margarine, cup, 1 T	60	60	0
Whipped Margarine, stick, 1 T	70	63	0
Miracle Whip® Light Reduced Calorie Salad Dressing, 1 T	45	36	5
Salad Dressing, 1 T	70	63	5
Mohawk Valley® Limburger Cheese, 1 oz	90	72	25
Limburger Pasteurized Process Cheese Spread, 1 oz	70	54	20
Molly McButter® sprinkles, ½ t	4	0	0
Morton® Beans & Frankfurters Dinner	343	117	28
Beef Pie	430	279	29
Chicken Pie	415	243	35
Fish Dinner	367	108	65
Ham Dinner	286	27	43
Meatloaf Dinner	306	153	48
Mexican Style Dinner	294	81	8
Salisbury Steak Dinner	294	153	37
Sliced Beef Dinner	215	36	65

	CAL	FAT (Cal)	CHOL (mg)
Spaghetti & Meatball Dinner	198	18	8
Turkey Pie	420	243	38
Turkey Dinner	226	54	45
Veal Parmigian Dinner	252	72	34
Western Dinner	289	117	31
Mr. Goodbar® chocolate bar, 1.85 oz	300	180	12
Muchos® Potato Crisps, 1 oz	150	81	0
Mueller's® Pasta Frills, 2 oz	210	9	0
Twists, 2 oz	210	9	0
Nabisco® Cream of Wheat®, Instant, 1.25 oz			
Apple 'N Cinnamon	130	0	0
w/ ¼ C 2% milk	160	10	5
Brown Sugar & Cinnamon	130	0	0
w/ ¼ C 2% milk	160	10	5
Maple Brown Sugar	130	0	0
w/ ¼ C 2% milk	160	10	5
Mixed Fruit	140	0	0
w/ ¼ C 2% milk	170	10	5
Original, 1 oz	100	0	0
w/ ¼ C 2% milk	130	10	5
Quick, 1 oz	100	0	0
w/ ¼ C 2% milk	130	10	5
Regular, 1 oz	100	0	0
w/ ¼ C 2% milk	130	10	5
Cream of Rice®, 1 oz	100	0	0
w/ ¼ C 2% milk	130	10	5
Frosted Wheat Squares®, 1 oz	100	0	0
w/ ½ C skim milk	143	2	0
w/ ½ C whole milk	178	40	18
Fruit Wheats®, 1 oz	100	0	0

	CAL	FAT (Cal)	CHOL (mg)
w/ ½ C skim milk	143	2	0
w/ ½ C whole milk	178	40	18
Shredded Wheat®, 1 oz	110	0	0
w/ ½ C skim milk	153	2	0
w/ ½ C whole milk	188	40	18
Shredded Wheat 'N Bran®, 1 oz	110	0	0
w/ ½ C skim milk	153	2	0
w/ ½ C whole milk	188	40	18
Nature Valley® Cinnamon & Raisin Granola, 1 oz	120	36	0
w/ ½ C skim milk	163	38	2
w/ ½ C whole milk	198	76	18
Coconut & Honey Granola, 1 oz	150	63	0
w/ ½ C skim milk	193	65	2
w/ ½ C whole milk	228	103	18
Fruit & Nut Granola, 1 oz	130	45	0
w/ ½ C skim milk	173	47	2
w/ ½ C whole milk	208	85	18
Toasted Oat Mixture Granola, 1 oz	130	45	0
w/ ½ C skim milk	173	47	2
w/ ½ C whole milk	208	85	18
Nature's Recipe® Bran 'n Honey, 1 slice	70	9	0
12 Grain, ⅔ slice	80	18	0
Noodle Roni®, Chicken Mushroom, 1.2 oz	134	22	19
prepared w/margarine and 2% milk	160	36	33
Fettucine, 1.5 oz	181	46	27
prepared w/margarine and 2% milk	300	162	33

	CAL	FAT (Cal)	CHOL (mg)
Garlic Butter, 1.5 oz	172	39	29
prepared w/margarine and 2% milk	300	153	38
Herb Butter, 1 oz	114	24	19
prepared w/margarine and 2% milk	160	63	28
Parmesano, 1.2 oz	135	26	19
prepared w/margarine and 2% milk	240	117	28
Pesto, 1.2 oz	131	19	NK
prepared w/margarine and 2% milk	220	108	NK
Romanoff, 1.5 oz	168	37	23
prepared w/margarine and 2% milk	240	99	32
Stroganoff, 2 oz	225	58	42
prepared w/margarine and 2% milk	350	153	60
Oatmeal Goodness® Cinnamon			
Oatmeal, 1 slice	90	18	0
Oatmeal & Bran, 1 slice	90	18	0
Oatmeal & Sunflower Seeds, 1 slice	90	18	0
Wheat Oatmeal, 1 slice	90	18	0
Ocean Spray® Cran-Apple, 6 fl oz	130	0	0
Cranberry Juice Cocktail, 6 fl oz	110	0	0
Cran-Grape, 6 fl oz	130	0	0
Cran-Raspberry, 6 fl oz	110	0	0
Mauna Lai, 6 fl oz	100	0	0
Pink Grapefruit Juice Cocktail, 6 fl oz	60	0	0
O'Gradys™ Extra Thick & Crunchy Crunchy Potato Chips, 1 oz	150	81	0

	CAL	FAT (Cal)	CHOL (mg)
Au Gratin Cheese Flavored, 1 oz	150	72	0
Hearty Seasonings, 1 oz	140	72	0
Open Pit® Barbecue Sauce			
Hickory Smoke Flavor, 1 T	25	0	0
Hot 'n Tangy Flavor, 1 T	25	0	0
Mesquite 'n Tangy Flavor, 1 T	25	0	0
Original Flavor, 1 T	25	0	0
Original Flavor w/Minced Onions, 1 T	25	0	0
Sweet 'n Tangy Flavor, 1 T	25	0	0
Thick 'n Tangy Hickory Flavor, 1 T	25	0	0
Ore-Ida® Cheddar Browns™, 3 oz	90	18	10
Chopped Onions, 2 oz	20	*1	0
Cob Corn, 1 ear	180	18	0
Cottage Fries, 3 oz	120	45	0
Country Style Dinner Fries, 3 oz	110	27	0
Crispers!®, 3 oz	230	135	0
Crispy Crowns!®, 3 oz	160	81	0
Crispy Crowns!® w/Onion, 3 oz	170	81	0
Golden Crinkles®, 3 oz	120	36	0
Golden Fries®, 3 oz	120	36	0
Golden Patties®, 2.5 oz	140	72	0
Home Style Potato Wedges™, 3 oz	100	27	0
Lites Crinkle Cuts, 3 oz	90	18	0
Lites French Fries, 3 oz	90	18	0
Lites Shoestrings, 3 oz	90	36	0

* Unreportable Amounts

	CAL	FAT (Cal)	CHOL (mg)
Microwave Crinkle Cuts, 3.5 oz	180	72	0
Microwave Hash Browns, 2 oz	130	72	0
Microwave Tater Tots®, 4 oz	200	81	0
Onion Ringers®, 2 oz	140	63	0
Pixie Crinkles®, 3 oz	140	54	0
Potatoes O'Brien, 3 oz	60	<9	0
Shoestrings, 3 oz	140	54	0
Shredded Hash Browns, 3 oz	70	<9	0
Small Whole Potatoes, 3 oz	70	<9	0
Stew Vegetables, 3 oz	60	<9	0
Tater Tots®, 3 oz	140	63	0
Tater Tots® w/Bacon Flavored Veg. Protein, 3 oz	140	54	0
Tater Tots® w/Onion, 3 oz	140	54	0
Vegetable Crisp® Broccoli, 3 oz	190	99	5
Vegetable Crisp® Cauliflower, 3 oz	150	81	5
Vegetable Crisp® Medley, 3 oz	160	81	5
Vegetable Crisp® Mushrooms, 2⅔ oz	130	63	5
Vegetable Crisp® Okra, 3 oz	160	81	5
Vegetable Crisp® Zucchini, 3 oz	150	81	5

Orville Redenbacher's® Butter Flavor Microwave Popping corn, 4 C

	CAL	FAT (Cal)	CHOL (mg)
Butter Flavor Microwave Popping corn, 4 C	110	54	0
Butter Flavor Salt Free Microwave Popping corn, 4 C	110	63	0
Caramel Microwave Popping Corn 2.5 C	240	126	9

	CAL	FAT (Cal)	CHOL (mg)
Cheddar Cheese Microwave Popping Corn, 3 C	150	90	1
Nacho Cheese Microwave Popping Corn, 3 C	140	81	2
Natural Flavor Salt Free Microwave Popping Corn, 4 C	120	72	0
Natural Flavor Microwave Popping Corn, 4 C	110	63	0
Original Oil & Salt Popping Corn, 4 C	160	72	0
Original Plain Popping Corn, 4 C	90	9	0
Sour Cream & Onion Microwave Popping Corn, 3 C	150	90	1
Ovaltine's® Classic Caffeine Free Malt, ¾ oz	80	0	0
Classic Chocolate Malt, ¾ oz	80	0	0
Hot 'N Rich® Hot cocoa Mix, 1 oz	120	27	0
50 Calorie, .45 oz	50	18	0
Sugar Free Mint, .41 oz	40	9	0
Parkay® Light Corn Oil Spread, 1 T	70	70	0
Margarine, 1 T	100	100	0
Soft Corn Oil Margarine, 1 T	100	100	0
Soft Margarine, 1 T	100	100	0
Soft Reduced Calorie Margarine, 1 T	50	50	0
Spread, 1 T	60	60	0
Squeeze® Margarine, 1 T	100	100	0
Whipped Margarine, tub, 1 T	60	60	0
Whipped Margarine, stick, 1 T	60	60	0

	CAL	FAT (Cal)	CHOL (mg)
Patio® Beef & Bean Burritos	487	171	22
Beef Bean Burritos	361	144	17
Beef Bean Green Burritos	333	117	18
Beef Bean Red Chili Burritos	330	108	14
Beef Enchilada Dinner	514	216	10
Burrito Dinner	517	144	7
Cheese Enchilada Dinner	378	81	5
Combination Dinner	468	189	9
Fiesta Dinner	461	180	8
Green Chili Burritos	488	171	23
Mexican Dinner	533	216	11
Nacho Beef Burritos	535	225	47
Nacho Cheese Burritos	485	171	36
Red Chili Burritos	477	180	23
Red Hot Burritos	352	135	15
Spicy Chicken Burritos	494	180	46
Peter Pan® Creamy Peanut Butter, 2 T	180	144	0
Crunchy Peanut Butter, 2 T	180	144	0
Salt Free Creamy Peanut Butter, 2 T	190	153	0
Salt Free Crunchy Peanut Butter, 2 T	180	153	0
Sodium Free Creamy Peanut Butter, 2 T	190	153	0
Philadelphia® Cream Cheese, 1 oz	100	90	30
w/Chives, 1 oz	90	81	30
w/Pimentos, 1 oz	90	81	30
Cream Cheese Product, light, 1 oz	60	45	15
Neufchatel Cheese, light, 1 oz	80	63	25
Soft Cream Cheese, 1 oz	100	90	30
w/Chives & Onion, 1 oz	100	72	30
w/Honey, 1 oz	100	72	25

	CAL	FAT (Cal)	CHOL (mg)
w/Olives & Pimento, 1 oz	90	72	30
w/Pineapple, 1 oz	90	72	25
w/Smoked Salmon, 1 oz	90	72	25
w/Strawberries, 1 oz	90	72	25
Whipped Cream Cheese, 1 oz	100	90	30
w/Bacon and Horseradish, 1 oz	90	81	20
w/Blue Cheese, 1 oz	100	81	25
w/Chives, 1 oz	90	81	25
w/Onions, 1 oz	90	72	20
w/Pimentos, 1 oz	90	72	20
w/Smoked Salmon, 1 oz	100	81	25
Pillsbury® Chocolate Frosting Supreme®, 1⅓ oz	150	54	0
Chocolate Fudge Frosting Supreme®, 1⅓ oz	150	54	0
Double Dutch Frosting Supreme®, 1⅓ oz	140	54	0
Idaho Mashed Potato, 1 serving of mix	70	0	0
prepared w/margarine & whole milk	130	54	4
Lemon Frosting Supreme®, 1⅓ oz	160	54	0
Microwave Bundt, ⅛ mix	180	36	0
prepared, ⅛ cake	270	117	35
Microwave Chocolate Cake Mix, ⅛ mix	120	27	0
prepared, ⅛ cake	210	117	35
Microwave Fudge Brownie Mix, 1 serving	130	27	0
prepared, 1 brownie	180	81	0
Microwave Lemon Cake Mix, ⅛ mix	120	27	0
prepared, ⅛ cake	220	117	34

	CAL	FAT (Cal)	CHOL (mg)
Microwave Yellow Cake,			
⅛ mix	120	27	0
prepared, ⅛ cake	220	117	35
Potato Pancake Mix, for			
3 pancakes	70	0	0
prepared, 3 pancakes	90	2	17
Strawberry Frosting			
Supreme®, 1⅓ oz	160	54	0
Polaner® Apricot All Fruit, 1 t	14	0	0
Blackberry All Fruit, 1 t	14	0	0
Black Cherry All Fruit, 1 t	14	0	0
Blueberry All Fruit, 1 t	14	0	0
Grape All Fruit, 1 t	14	0	0
Orange All Fruit, 1 t	14	0	0
Peach All Fruit, 1 t	14	0	0
Raspberry All Fruit, 1 t	14	0	0
Strawberry All Fruit, 1 t	14	0	0
Post® Alpha-Bits®, 1 oz	110	9	0
w/ ½ C skim milk	153	11	2
w/ ½ C whole milk	188	49	18
C.W. Post® Hearty Granola			
Cereal, 1 oz	130	36	0
w/ ½ C skim milk	173	38	2
w/ ½ C whole milk	208	76	18
w/Raisins, 1 oz	120	36	0
w/ ½ C skim milk	163	38	2
w/ ½ C whole milk	198	76	18
Cocoa Pebbles®, 1 oz	110	9	0
w/ ½ C skim milk	153	11	2
w/ ½ C whole milk	188	49	18
Fortified Oat Flakes, 1 oz	110	9	0
w/ ½ C skim milk	153	11	2
w/ ½ C whole milk	188	49	18
Fruit & Fiber® Dates,			
Raisins, Walnuts, 1 oz	90	9	0

	CAL	FAT (Cal)	CHOL (mg)
w/ ½ C skim milk	133	11	2
w/ ½ C whole milk	168	49	18
Harvest Medley, 1 oz	90	9	0
w/ ½ C skim milk	133	11	2
w/ ½ C whole milk	168	49	18
Mountain Trail, 1 oz	90	9	0
w/ ½ C skim milk	133	11	2
w/ ½ C whole milk	168	49	18
Tropical Fruit, 1 oz	90	9	0
w/ ½ C skim milk	133	11	2
w/ ½ C whole milk	168	49	18
Fruity Pebbles®, 1 oz	110	9	0
w/ ½ C skim milk	153	11	2
w/ ½ C whole milk	188	49	18
Grape-Nuts®, 1 oz	110	0	0
w/ ½ C skim milk	153	2	2
w/ ½ C whole milk	188	40	18
Grape-Nuts® Flakes, 1 oz	100	9	0
w/ ½ C skim milk	143	11	2
w/ ½ C whole milk	178	49	18
Honeycomb®, 1 oz	110	0	0
w/ ½ C skim milk	153	2	2
w/ ½ C whole milk	188	40	18
Natural Bran Flakes, 1 oz	90	0	0
w/ ½ C skim milk	133	2	2
w/ ½ C whole milk	168	40	18
Natural Raisin Bran, 1 oz	80	0	0
w/ ½ C skim milk	123	2	2
w/ ½ C whole milk	158	40	18
Post Toasties® Corn Flakes, 1 oz	110	0	0
w/ ½ C skim milk	153	2	2
w/ ½ C whole milk	188	40	18
Raisin Grape-Nuts®, 1 oz	100	0	0
w/ ½ C skim milk	143	2	2
w/ ½ C whole milk	178	40	18
Smurf-Berry Crunch®, 1 oz	110	9	0

	CAL	FAT (Cal)	CHOL (mg)
w/ ½ C skim milk	153	11	2
w/ ½ C whole milk	188	49	18
Super Golden Crisp®, 1 oz	110	0	0
w/ ½ C skim milk	153	2	2
w/ ½ C whole milk	188	40	18
Postum® Coffee Flavor Instant Hot Beverage, 6 fl oz	12	0	0
Instant Hot Beverage, 6 fl oz	12	0	0
Presto® Italian Dressing, 1 T	70	63	0
Prego® Marinara Sauce, 4 oz	136	45	0
Spaghetti Sauce, 4 oz	100	45	0
No-Salt-Added, 4 oz	100	45	0
w/Mushrooms, 4 oz	133	45	0
Princella® Mashed Yams, canned, ½ C	90	0	0
Yams in Heavy Syrup, canned, ½ C	120	0	0
Yams in Light Syrup, canned, ½ C	110	0	0
Yams in Pineapple Orange Sauce, canned, ½ C	190	0	0
Pringle's® Potato Chips, 1 oz	170	117	0
Cheez-ums, 1 oz	170	117	0
Idaho Rippled French Onion, 1 oz	170	108	0
Idaho Rippled Original, 1 oz	170	108	0
Idaho Rippled Taco 'n Cheddar	170	108	0
Light, 1 oz	150	72	0
Light B-B-Q, 1 oz	150	72	0
Light Ranch, 1 oz	150	72	0

	CAL	FAT (Cal)	CHOL (mg)
Puritan Oil®, 1 T	120	120	0
Quaker® Bran, unprocessed, 0.25 oz	8	2	0
Captain Crunch®, 1 oz	113	15	0
w/ ½ C skim milk	156	17	2
w/ ½ C whole milk	191	55	18
Cap'n Crunch Crunchberries®, 1 oz	113	15	0
w/ ½ C skim milk	156	17	2
w/ ½ C whole milk	191	55	18
Cap'n Crunch® Peanut Butter, 1 oz	119	27	0
w/ ½ C skim milk	162	29	2
w/ ½ C whole milk	197	67	18
Caramel Nut Dipps®, 1.1 oz	148	58	2
Chocolate Chip Chewy Granola Bar, 1 oz	128	42	.3
Chocolate Chip Dipps®, 1 oz	139	57	1
Chocolate Graham & Marshmallow Chewy Granola Bar, 1 oz	126	40	.3
Chunky Nut & Raisin Chewy Granola Bar, 1 oz	131	52	.2
Cinnamon Life®, 1 oz	101	15	0
w/ ½ C skim milk	144	17	2
w/ ½ C whole milk	179	55	18
Crunchy Bran®, 1 oz	89	12	0
w/ ½ C skim milk	132	14	2
w/ ½ C whole milk	167	52	18
Crunchy Nut Ohs®, 1 oz	127	38	0
w/ ½ C skim milk	170	40	2
w/ ½ C whole milk	205	78	18
Honey & Oats Chewy Granola Bar, 1 oz	125	40	.3
Honey Graham Ohs®, 1 oz	122	29	0

	CAL	FAT (Cal)	CHOL (mg)
w/ ½ C skim milk	165	31	2
w/ ½ C whole milk	200	69	18
Instant Oats, 1 oz	94	18	0
Apple Cinnamon, 1.25 oz	118	14	0
Banana & Cream, 1.25 oz	131	21	0
Blueberries & Cream, 1.25 oz	131	22	0
Cinnamon Spice, 1.63 oz	164	19	0
Maple & Brown Sugar, 1.5 oz	152	19	0
Peaches & Cream, 1.25 oz	129	20	0
Raisin Date Walnut, 1.3 oz	141	34	0
Raisin Spice, 1.5 oz	149	18	0
Strawberries & Cream, 1.25 oz	129	18	0
King Vitamin®, 1 oz	110	9	0
w/ ½ C skim milk	153	11	2
w/ ½ C whole milk	188	49	18
Life®, 1 oz	101	15	0
w/ ½ C skim milk	144	17	2
w/ ½ C whole milk	179	55	18
Oat Bran, 1 oz	92	19	0
Oat Squares®, 1 oz	105	14	0
w/ ½ C skim milk	148	16	2
w/ ½ C whole milk	183	54	18
Old Fashioned Oats, 1 oz	99	18	0
100% Natural® Cereal, 1 oz	127	50	0
w/ ½ C skim milk	170	52	2
w/ ½ C whole milk	205	90	18
Apple Cinnamon, 1 oz	126	44	0
w/ ½ C skim milk	169	46	2
w/ ½ C whole milk	204	84	18
Raisin Date, 1 oz	123	45	0
w/ ½ C skim milk	166	47	2
w/ ½ C whole milk	201	85	18
Peanut Butter Chewy Granola Bar, 1 oz	128	44	.3

	CAL	FAT (Cal)	CHOL (mg)
Peanut Butter Chocolate Chip Chewy Granola Bar, 1 oz	131	51	.3
Peanut Butter Dipps®, 1.15 oz	170	82	2
Popeye Sweet Crunch®, 1 oz	113	16	0
w/ ½ C skim milk	156	18	2
w/ ½ C whole milk	191	56	18
Puffed Rice®, 0.5 oz	54	1	0
w/ ½ C skim milk	97	3	2
w/ ½ C whole milk	132	40	18
Puffed Wheat, 0.5 oz	50	2	0
w/ ½ C skim milk	93	4	2
w/ ½ C whole milk	128	42	18
Quick Oats, 1 oz	99	18	0
Raisin Cinnamon Chewy Granola Bar, 1 oz	128	45	.3
Rice Cakes, Barley & Oats, 0.32 oz	34	3	0
Buckwheat, 0.32 oz	35	3	0
Corn, 0.32 oz	35	3	0
Corn Grain, 0.32 oz	35	2	0
Multi-Grain, 0.32 oz	34	4	0
Multi-Grain, Salt-Free, 0.32 oz	35	4	0
Plain, 0.32 oz	35	3	0
Plain, unsalted, 0.32 oz	35	3	0
Rye, 0.32 oz	34	4	0
Rye Grain, 0.32 oz	35	3	0
Sesame, 0.32 oz	35	3	0
Sesame, Salt-Free, 0.32	35	3	0
Wheat Grain, 0.32 oz	34	3	0
Shredded Wheat, 1.4 oz	132	5	0
w/ ½ C skim milk	175	7	2
w/ ½ C whole milk	210	45	18
Whole Wheat Hot Natural Cereal, 1 oz	92	5	0

	CAL	FAT (Cal)	CHOL (mg)
Ralston® Almond Delight®, 1 oz	110	18	0
w/ ½ C skim milk	153	20	2
w/ ½ C whole milk	188	58	18
Bran Chex®, 1 oz	90	0	0
w/ ½ C skim milk	133	2	2
w/ ½ C whole milk	168	40	18
Bran News®, Apple, 1 oz	100	9	0
w/ ½ C skim milk	143	11	2
w/ ½ C whole milk	178	49	18
Cinnamon, 1 oz	100	9	0
w/ ½ C skim milk	143	11	2
w/ ½ C whole milk	178	49	18
Corn Chex®, 1 oz	110	0	0
w/ ½ C skim milk	153	9	2
w/ ½ C whole milk	188	40	18
Crunch Berries®, 1 oz	120	36	0
w/ ½ C skim milk	163	38	2
w/ ½ C whole milk	198	76	18
Dinersaurs, 1 oz	110	9	0
w/ ½ C skim milk	153	11	2
w/ ½ C whole milk	188	49	18
Double Chex, 1 oz	100	0	0
w/ ½ C skim milk	143	2	2
w/ ½ C whole milk	178	40	18
Dunkin' Donuts® Cereal, 1 oz	120	9	0
w/ ½ C skim milk	163	11	2
w/ ½ C whole milk	198	49	18
Freakies®, 1 oz	110	9	0
w/ ½ C skim milk	153	11	2
w/ ½ C whole milk	188	49	18
Honey Graham Chex®, 1 oz	110	9	0
w/ ½ C skim milk	153	11	2
w/ ½ C whole milk	188	49	18
Muesli®, Raisins, Dates, & almonds, 1.45 oz	160	27	0
w/ ½ C skim milk	203	29	2

	CAL	FAT (Cal)	CHOL (mg)
w/ ½ C whole milk	238	67	18
Raisins, Peaches, & Pecans, 1.45 oz	160	27	0
w/ ½ C skim milk	203	29	2
w/ ½ C whole milk	238	67	18
Peanut Butter Crunch®, 1 oz	120	27	0
w/ ½ C skim milk	163	29	2
w/ ½ C whole milk	198	67	18
Rice Chex®, 1 oz	110	0	0
w/ ½ C skim milk	153	2	2
w/ ½ C whole milk	188	40	18
Wheat Chex®, 1 oz	100	0	0
w/ ½ C skim milk	143	2	2
w/ ½ C whole milk	178	40	18
Red Band® Plain all-Purpose flour, 1 C	390	9	0
Self-Rising flour, 1 C	380	9	0
Whole Wheat Blend, 1 C	400	18	0
Reese's® Peanut Butter Cup, 1.8 oz	280	153	8
Peanut Butter Flavored Chips, 1.5 oz	230	117	3
Pieces, 1.95 oz	270	99	2
Reymond's® 'taliano, 2 slices	150	18	0
Triti-Kay Natural Grain, 1 slice	90	<9	0
Rice-A-Roni® Beef Flavor, 1.33 oz	135	8	1
prepared as directed	170	45	6
Brown Wild Rice, 1.16 oz	121	14	1
prepared as directed	180	72	6
Chicken Flavor, 1.33 oz	136	8	1
prepared as directed	170	45	6
Chicken Mushroom, 1.25 oz	129	11	1

	CAL	FAT (Cal)	CHOL (mg)
prepared as directed	180	63	6
Chicken Vegetable, 1.2 oz	124	8	1
prepared as directed	150	36	6
Fried Chinese, 1.04 oz	106	8	.3
prepared as directed	140	45	5
Herb Butter Rice, 1.04 oz	105	7	1
prepared as directed	140	36	6
Long Grain & Wild, 1 oz	100	3	.3
prepared as directed	140	36	5
Pilaf Rice (Savory), 1.45 oz	147	8	1
prepared as directed	190	56	6
Risotto Rice, 1.5 oz	157	13	2
prepared as directed	200	54	7
Savory Broccoli Au gratin, 1.12 oz	129	31	4
prepared w/margarine	180	63	4
Savory Cauliflower Au gratin, 1.2 oz	141	32	5
prepared w/margarine	170	63	5
Savory Chicken Florentine, 1.07 oz	108	7	.5
prepared w/margarine	130	36	.5
Savory Creamy Parmesan & Herb, 1.22 oz	145	38	7
prepared w/margarine	170	63	7
Savory Garden Pilaf, 1.12 oz	113	7	1
prepared w/margarine	140	36	1
Savory Spring Vegetable & Cheese, 1.22 oz	141	32	6
prepared w/margarine	170	63	6
Savory Zesty Cheddar, 1.3 oz	151	34	6
prepared w/margarine	180	63	6
Spanish Style, 1 07 oz	107	5	.5
prepared as directed	150	36	6
Stroganoff Rice, 1.35 oz	150	27	5
prepared as directed	190	72	10

	CAL	FAT (Cal)	CHOL (mg)
Yellow Rice, 2 oz	196	5	.6
prepared as directed	250	63	6
Roka® Blue Cheese Dressing, 1 T	60	6	10
Blue Cheese Reduced Calorie Dressing, 1 T	14	9	5
Blue Spread, 1 oz	70	54	20
Rolo® Caramels, 1.93 oz	270	108	13
Rold Gold® Pretzel Rods, 1 oz	110	18	0
Pretzel Sticks, 1 oz	110	9	0
Pretzel Twists, 1 oz	110	9	0
Roman Meal® Light Wheat, 1 slice	40	<9	0
Light White, 1 slice	40	<9	0
Ronzoni® Cavatelli, 2 oz	210	9	0
Ditalini, 2 oz	210	9	0
Elbows, 2 oz	210	9	0
Fusilli, 2 oz	210	9	0
Lasagne, 2 oz	210	9	0
Linguini, 2 oz	210	9	0
Manicotti, 2 oz	210	9	0
Mezzani Rigati, 2 oz	210	9	0
Mostaccioli Rigati, 2 oz	210	9	0
Perciatelli, 2 oz	210	9	0
Shells, 2 oz	210	9	0
Spaghetti, 2 oz	210	9	0
Spinach Rotelle, 2 oz	210	9	0
Tri-Color Radiatore, 2 oz	210	9	0
Tri-Color Rigatini, 2 oz	210	9	0
Vermicelli, 2 oz	210	9	0
Ziti Rigati, 2 oz	210	9	0

	CAL	FAT (Cal)	CHOL (mg)
Royal® Cherry Gelatin, ½ C	80	0	0
Chocolate Instant Pudding & Pie Filling, mix	120	9	0
prepared w/skim milk, ½ C	163	11	2
prepared w/whole milk, ½ C	218	49	18
Chocolate Pudding & Pie Filling, mix	120	9	0
prepared w/skim milk, ½ C	163	11	2
prepared w/whole milk, ½ C	218	49	18
Dark 'n' Sweet Chocolate Pudding & Pie Filling, mix	120	9	0
prepared w/skim milk, ½ C	163	11	2
prepared w/whole milk, ½ C	218	49	18
Orange Gelatin, ½ C	80	0	0
Raspberry Gelatin, ½ C	80	0	0
Strawberry/Banana Gelatin, ½ C	80	0	0
Vanilla Pudding & Pie Filling, mix	80	9	0
prepared w/skim milk, ½ C	123	11	2
prepared w/whole milk, ½ C	158	49	18
Royal Prince® Mashed Yams, canned, ½ C	90	0	0
Yams in Heavy Syrup, canned, ½ C	120	0	0
Yams in Light Syrup, canned, ½ C	110	0	0

	CAL	FAT (Cal)	CHOL (mg)
Yams in Pineapple Orange Sauce, canned, ½ C	190	0	0
Ruffles® Potato Chips, 1 oz	150	90	0
Bar-B-Q Flavored, 1 oz	150	81	0
Cajun Spice Flavored, 1 oz	150	90	0
Cheddar & Sour Cream Flavored, 1 oz	150	81	0
Sour Cream & Onion Flavored, 1 oz	150	81	0
San Giorgio® Capellini, 2 oz	210	9	0
Cut Ziti, 2 oz	210	9	0
Elbow Macaroni, 2 oz	210	9	0
Lasagne, 2 oz	210	9	0
Linguini, 2 oz	210	9	0
Rotelle, 2 oz	210	9	0
Rigatoni, 2 oz	210	9	0
Small Rigatoni, 2 oz	210	9	0
Spaghetti, 2 oz	210	9	0
Sanalac® Non-Fat Dry Milk, 4 T	80	<9	4
Santitas™ Restaurant Style Tortilla Chips, 1 oz	140	54	0
Strips, 1 oz	140	63	0
Sauceworks® Cocktail Sauce, 1 T	12	0	0
Horseradish Sauce, 1 T	50	45	5
Hot Mustard Sauce, 1 T	35	18	5
Natural Lemon & Herb Flavor Tartar Sauce, 1 T	70	70	5
Sweet'N Sour Sauce, 1 T	20	0	0
Tartar Sauce, 1 T	70	70	5
Seneca® Grape Juice, 6 oz	120	0	0

	CAL	FAT (Cal)	CHOL (mg)
Sensible Chef® Beef Pepper Steak			
w/Rice	250	90	21
Beef Stroganoff w/Gravy	240	72	27
Beef Tip w/Vegetables &			
Noodles	250	81	20
Chicken & Dumplings	330	144	23
Chicken a la King w/Rice	250	72	19
Fettucini al Fredo w/Chicken	410	198	22
Lasagna w/Meat Sauce	390	171	26
Linguini w/Shrimp & Clams	190	27	18
Swedish Meatballs w/Gravy	360	144	22
Shake 'N Bake® Country Mild			
Seasoning, ¼ pouch	80	36	0
Homestyle Oven Fry for			
Chicken, ¼ pouch	80	18	0
Oven Fry® for Chicken,			
¼ pouch	110	18	0
for Pork	120	27	0
Italian Herb Seasoning,			
¼ pouch	80	9	0
Original Barbeque Seasoning			
for Chicken,	80	18	0
for Fish	70	9	0
for Pork	80	9	0
Original Barbecue Seasoning			
for Chicken,			
¼ pouch	90	18	0
for Pork	80	18	0
Smokelle® Pasteurized Process			
Cheese Food, 1 oz	100	63	20
Smuckers® Apricot Preserves, 1 t	18	0	0
Low Sugar Concord Grape			
Spread, 1 t	8	0	0

	CAL	FAT (Cal)	CHOL (mg)
Orange Marmalade			
Spread, 1 t	8	0	0
Strawberry Spread, 1 t	8	0	0
Orange Marmalade, 1 t	18	0	0
Red Raspberry Preserves, 1 t	18	0	0
Simply Fruit Blueberry, 1 t	16	0	0
Concord Grape, 1 t	16	0	0
Orange Marmalade, 1 t	16	0	0
Red Raspberry, 1 t	16	0	0
Strawberry, 1 t	16	0	0
Strawberry Preserves, 1 t	18	0	0
Snack Pack® Apple Sauce, 4.25 oz	80	0	0
Natural, 4.25 oz	50	0	0
Strawberry Apple Sauce,			
4.25 oz	80	0	0
Raspberry Apple Sauce,			
4.25 oz	80	0	0
Softasilk® flour, ¼ C	100	0	0
Sorrell Ridge® Black Raspberry			
Conserve, 1 t	13	0	0
Boysenberry Conserve, 1 t	13	0	0
Cherry Conserve, 1 t	13	0	0
Concord Grape Conserve, 1 t	14	0	0
Cranberry Sauce, 1 t	14	0	0
Orange Marmalade, 1 t	13	0	0
Peach Conserve, 1 t	13	0	0
Plum Good! Conserve, 1 t	14	0	0
Raspberry Conserve, 1 t	13	0	0
Strawberry Conserve, 1 t	13	0	0
Strawberry Rhubarb			
Conserve, 1 t	13	0	0
Wild Blueberry Conserve, 1 t	13	0	0

	CAL	FAT (Cal)	CHOL (mg)
Squeeze-A-Snak® Garlic Flavor Pasteurized Processed Cheese Spread, 1 oz	90	63	20
Hickory Smoke Flavor Pasteurized Processed Cheese Spread, 1 oz	80	63	20
Pasteurized Processed Cheese Spread			
w/Bacon, 1 oz	90	63	20
w/Pimento, 1 oz	90	63	20
Sharp Pasteurized Processed Cheese Spread, 1 oz	80	63	20
Stouffer's® Lean Cuisine Baked Rigatoni	260	90	35
Beef & Pork Cannelloni	270	90	45
Breast of Chicken Marsala	190	45	65
Cheese Cannelloni	270	90	30
Chicken a l'Orange	270	45	50
Chicken & Vegetables	270	63	45
Chicken Cacciatore	280	90	45
Chicken Chow Mein	250	45	30
Filet of Fish Divan	270	81	90
Filet of Fish Florentine	240	81	100
Filet of Fish Jardiniere	280	90	95
Glazed Chicken	270	72	60
Herbed Lamb	270	72	60
Linguini with Clam Sauce	260	63	30
Meatball Stew	250	90	80
Oriental Beef	270	72	45
Salisbury Steak	270	117	5
Shrimp and Chicken Cantonese	260	81	105
Sliced Turkey Breast	220	45	50
Spaghetti	280	63	25
Stuffed Cabbage	220	81	40
Szechwan Beef	280	99	90

	CAL	FAT (Cal)	CHOL (mg)
Tuna Lasagna	280	90	25
Turkey Dijon	280	90	65
Veal Lasagna	280	72	75
Veal Primavera	250	81	80
Vegetable & Pasta Mornay	280	117	45
Zucchini Lasagna	260	63	20
Stove Top® Stuffing Mix			
Americana® New England	110	9	0
prepared w/butter, ½ C	180	81	20
Americana® San Francisco	110	9	0
prepared w/butter, ½ C	170	81	20
Beef	110	9	0
prepared w/butter, ½ C	180	81	20
Chicken Flavor	110	9	0
prepared w/butter, ½ C	180	81	20
Chicken Flavor Flexible			
Stuffing	120	27	0
prepared w/butter, ½ C	170	81	15
Cornbread	110	9	0
prepared w/butter, ½ C	170	81	20
Cornbread Flavor Flexible			
Stuffing	120	27	0
prepared w/butter, ½ C	170	72	15
Homestyle Herb Flexible			
Stuffing	120	27	0
prepared w/butter, ½ C	170	81	15
Long Grain & Wild Rice	120	9	0
prepared w/butter, ½ C	180	81	20
Pork	110	9	0
prepared w/butter, ½ C	170	81	20
Savory Herbs	110	9	0
prepared w/butter, ½ C	180	81	20
Turkey	110	9	0
prepared w/butter, ½ C	170	81	20
With Rice	110	9	0
prepared w/butter, ½ C	180	81	20

	CAL	FAT (Cal)	CHOL (mg)
Sun Country® Granola Raisin Date,			
1 oz	123	41	0
w/ ½ C skim milk	166	43	2
w/ ½ C whole milk	201	81	18
Granola w/Almonds, 1 oz	130	48	0
w/ ½ C skim milk	173	50	2
w/ ½ C whole milk	108	88	18
Granola w/Raisins, 1 oz	125	43	0
w/ ½ C skim milk	168	45	2
w/ ½ C whole milk	203	83	18
Sun Main® Apple Chunks, dried,			
2 oz	150	0	0
Apricots, dried, 1 oz	140	0	0
Calimyrna Figs, dried, ½ C	250	18	0
Fruit Bits, dried, 2 oz	160	<9	0
Golden Raisins, ½ C	260	0	0
Mission Figs, dried, ½ C	210	9	0
Peaches, dried, 2 oz	140	0	0
Raisins, ½ C	250	0	0
Sunshine® American Heritage®			
Cheddar snack crackers, 5	80	36	5
Parmesan snack crackers,			
4	70	36	tr
Sesame snack crackers, 4	70	36	0
Wheat snack crackers, 4	60	27	0
Animal Crackers, 14	120	27	0
Bite Size Shredded Wheat			
Cereal, ⅔ C	110	9	0
with ½ C skim milk	153	11	2
with ½ C whole milk	188	49	18
Butter Flavored Cookies, 4	120	45	5
Cheez-It® Snack crackers, 12	70	36	0
Chip-A-Roos® cookies, 2	130	63	tr
Chips'n Middles™ cookies, 2	140	54	tr

	CAL	FAT (Cal)	CHOL (mg)
Chocolate Fudge Sandwich Cookies, 2	150	63	0
Cinnamon Graham Crackers, 4	70	27	0
Country Style Oatmeal cookies, 2	110	45	0
Cup Custard, 2	130	54	5
Fig Bars, 2	90	18	0
Ginger Snaps, 5	100	27	0
Golden Fruit Raisin Biscuits, 2	150	27	0
Graham Cracker Crumbs, 1 C	550	126	0
Hi Ho® crackers, 4	80	45	tr
Honey Graham Crackers, 4	60	18	0
Hydrox® cookies, 3	160	63	0
Krispy® Saltine crackers, 5	60	9	0
Unsalted Tops crackers, 5	60	9	0
Lemon Coolers Cookies, 5	140	54	0
Mallopuffs, 2	140	36	0
Oatmeal Peanut Sandwich Cookies, 2	140	54	0
Oyster & Soup Crackers, 16	60	18	0
Peanut Butter Wafers, 3	120	54	0
Shredded Wheat Cereal, 1 biscuit	90	9	0
w/ ½ C skim milk	133	11	2
w/ ½ C whole milk	168	49	18
Sprinkles, 2	130	27	0
Sugar Wafers, 3	130	54	0
Vanilla Wafers, 6	130	54	5
Vienna Finger Sandwich® cookies, 2	140	54	0
Wheat Wafers, 8	80	36	0
Sunsweet® Apricots, dried, 2 oz	140	0	0
Large Prunes, dried, 2 oz	120	0	0

	CAL	FAT (Cal)	CHOL (mg)
Medium Prunes, dried, 2 oz	120	0	0
Pitted Prunes, dried, 2 oz	140	0	0
Prune Juice, 6 fl oz	130	0	0
Prune Juice w Prune/Pulp, 6 fl oz	130	0	0
Ready to Serve Prunes, ½ C	120	0	0
Sunbeam® bread, 1 slice	60	<9	0
Lite White, 1 slice	40	<9	tr
Butter Top Wheat, 2 slices	140	9	0
Sweet 'n Low®, 1 packet	4	0	0
Swiss Miss® Butterscotch Pudding, 4 oz	160	54	1
Chocolate Pudding, 4 oz	180	54	1
Chocolate Fudge Pudding, 4 oz	170	54	1
Double Rich Hot Cocoa Mix	110	27	.2
made w/6 fl oz skim milk	142	29	2
Hot Cocoa Mix w/Mini Marshmallows	110	27	.2
made w/6 fl oz skim milk	142	29	2
Lite Hot Cocoa Mix	70	<9	1
made w/6 fl oz skim milk	102	<11	3
Milk Chocolate Hot Cocoa Mix	110	27	.2
made w/6 fl oz skim milk	142	29	2
Sugar Free Hot Cocoa Mix	50	<9	1
made w/6 fl oz skim milk	82	<11	3
Sugar Free Hot Cocoa Mix w/Marshmallow flavor	50	<9	1
made w/6 fl oz skim milk	82	<11	3
Tapioca Pudding, 4 oz	150	36	1
Vanilla Sundae Pudding, 4 oz	160	54	1

	CAL	FAT (Cal)	CHOL (mg)
Tang® Breakfast Beverage Crystals, 6 fl oz	90	0	0
Sugar Free Breakfast Beverage Crystals, 6 fl oz	6	0	0
Tostitos® Jalapeno & Cheese Flavored Tortilla Chips, 1 oz	150	72	0
Sharp Nacho Cheese Flavored Tortilla Chips, 1 oz	150	72	0
Tortilla Chips, 1 oz	140	72	0
Tootsie Roll®, 1 oz	112	23	tr
Flavor Roll, 1 oz	117	22	tr
Tootsie Pop, 0.6 oz	66	.5	tr
Tyson® All White Cooked Fryer Meat, 3.5 oz	166	31	40
Batter Gold Chicken, 3.5 oz	285	168	85
Boneless Breast, 3.5 oz	205	113	50
Breast of Chicken Roll, 3.5 oz	155	84	47
Breast Strips, 3.5 oz	270	120	43
Buttermilk Chicken, 3.5 oz	285	176	71
Chicken Bologna, 3.5 oz	230	163	60
Chicken Cordon Blue, 3.5 oz	225	115	38
Chicken Corn Dogs, 3.5 oz	280	130	55
Chicken Franks, 3.5 oz	285	224	68
Chicken Kiev, 3.5 oz	90	194	73
Chicken Pattie, 3.5 oz	275	167	58
Cornish & Split Cornish, 3.5 oz	240	128	52
Delecta Delicious Chicken, 3.5 oz	305	172	82
Heat N Serve Chicken, 3.5 oz	270	150	74

	CAL	FAT (Cal)	CHOL (mg)
Heat N Serve, 3.5 oz	280	170	53
Honey Stung Chicken, 3.5 oz	260	128	90
IQF Chickens & Split Broilers, 3.5 oz	245	132	58
Liberty Roll, 3.5 oz	185	104	53
Lightly Breaded Chicken, 3.5 oz	255	128	94
Natural Proportioned Cooked Chicken Meat, 3.5 oz	170	44	53
Prebreaded Marinated Chicken, 3.5 oz	285	156	65
Sandwich Mate, 3.5 oz	315	176	40
School Lunch Pattie, 3.5 oz	290	177	33
Stuffed Breast, 3.5 oz	160	60	34
Velveeta® Mexican Pasteurized Processed Cheese Spread, hot, 1 oz	80	54	20
mild, 1 oz	80	54	20
Pasteurized Processed Cheese Spread, 1 oz	80	54	20
Pimento, 1 oz	80	54	20
Slices Pasteurized Processed Cheese Spread, 1 oz	90	54	20
Shells & Cheese Dinner, ¾ C	260	90	25
Very Fine® Grape Drink, 8 fl oz	130	0	0
Vlasic® Kosher Dill Spears, 1 oz	30	0	0
Old Fashioned Bread & Butter Chunks, 1 oz	25	0	0
Polish Dill Spears, 1 oz	4	0	0
Sweet Chunky Relish, 1 oz	30	0	0
Sweet Gherkins, 1 oz	45	0	0

	CAL	FAT (Cal)	CHOL (mg)
Weight Watchers® Apple Pie, 1 slice	190	45	10
Apple Sweet Roll, 1	190	45	15
Baked Cheese Ravioli	310	108	50
Beef Enchiladas Ranchero	310	117	90
Beef Fajitas	270	63	30
Beef Salisbury Steak Romana	320	117	80
Beef Stroganoff	340	135	95
Beefsteak Burrito	330	108	80
Black Forest Cake, 1 serving	180	45	<5
Boston Cream Pie, 1 serving	170	36	5
Broccoli and Cheese Baked Potato	280	63	30
Carrot Cake, 1 serving	170	54	10
Cheese Enchiladas Ranchero	370	198	105
Cheese Manicotti	300	117	75
Cheese French Bread Pizza	320	99	45
Cheese Pizza	320	72	45
Cheesecake, 1 serving	220	63	25
Chicken Ala King	230	72	60
Chicken Burrito	330	126	65
Chicken Divan Baked Potato	300	54	30
Chicken Enchiladas Suiza	360	153	70
Chicken Fajitas	260	54	30
Chicken Fettucini	300	90	85
Chicken Nuggets, 4 nuggets	180	99	55
Chicken Patty Parmigiana	280	144	85
Chocolate Brownie, 1	100	36	10
Chocolate Cake, 1 serving	180	45	5
Chocolate Ice Milk, 4.6 oz	100	27	10
Chocolate Mousse, 1 serving	170	54	10
Chopped Beef Steak	280	153	100
Deluxe Combination Pizza	300	72	35
Deluxe French Bread Pizza	330	108	30
Fillet of Fish au Gratin	210	54	85
German Chocolate Cake, 1 serving	190	63	10

	CAL	FAT (Cal)	CHOL (mg)
Imperial Chicken	230	36	60
Italian Cheese Lasagna	370	126	60
Lasagna with Meat Sauce	340	126	70
Neopolitan Ice Milk, 4.6 oz	100	27	10
Oven Fried Fish	220	108	50
Pasta Primavera	290	117	15
Pasta Rigati	290	72	45
Pepperoni French Bread Pizza	330	117	50
Pepperoni Pizza	320	81	50
Pound Cake with Blueberry Topping, 1 serving	180	54	15
Raspberry Mousse, 1 serving	160	54	20
Sausage Pizza	310	72	40
Seafood Linguini	220	72	5
Southern Fried Chicken Patty	270	144	70
Spaghetti with Meat Sauce	280	63	20
Strawberry Cheesecake, 1 serving	180	45	20
Strawberry Shortcake, 1 serving	160	36	0
Stuffed Sole with Newburg Sauce	310	81	5
Stuffed Turkey Breast	270	90	90
Sweet 'n Sour Chicken Tenders	250	18	45
Vanilla Ice Milk, 4.6 oz	100	27	10
Veal Patty Parmigiana	240	99	55
Welch's® Grape Juice, 6 fl oz	120	0	0
White Grape Juice, 6 fl oz	110	0	0
Wheatena®, 1 oz	100	0	0
White Deer® All-Purpose Flour, 1 C	400	9	0

	CAL	FAT (Cal)	CHOL (mg)
Wise® Barbecue Potato Chips, 1 oz	150	90	0
Butter Popcorn, ½ oz	80	45	0
Cottage Fries, 1 oz	160	99	0
Dipsy Doodle® Corn Chips, 1 oz	160	90	0
Lightly Salted Potato Chips, 1 oz	160	99	0
Onion Flavor Rings, 1 oz	130	45	0
Onion Garlic Potato Chips, 1 oz	150	90	0
Potato Chips, 1 oz	160	126	0
Ridges, 1 oz	160	99	0
Salt & Vinegar Potato Chips, 1 oz	160	99	0
Spirals, 1 oz	160	90	0
Wish Bone® Blended Italian Dressing, 1 T	40	36	0
Chunky Blue Cheese Dressing, 1 T	70	72	tr
Creamy Garlic Dressing, 1 T	80	72	0
Creamy Dijon Dressing, 1 T	60	54	5
Creamy Italian Dressing, 1 T	60	45	tr
Deluxe French Dressing, 1 T	60	54	0
Dijon Vinaigrette Dressing, 1 T	60	54	0
Garlic French Dressing, 1 T	60	54	0
Herbal Italian Dressing, 1 T	70	63	0
Italian Dressing, 1 T	40	36	0
Italian w/Cheese, 1 T	60	54	0
Lite Blue Cheese Dressing, 1 T	40	36	tr
Creamy Dijon Dressing, 1 T	25	18	5
Dijon Vinaigrette Dressing, 1 T	25	18	0
French Style Dressing, 1 T	30	18	0

	CAL	FAT (Cal)	CHOL (mg)
Italian Dressing, 1 T	6	0	0
Onion & Chive Dressing, 1 T	35	27	0
Ranch Dressing, 1 T	45	36	5
Russian Dressing, 1 T	20	<9	0
Sweet 'N Spicy French Style, 1 T	18	<9	0
Thousand Island Dressing, 1 T	40	27	10
Ranch Dressing, 1 T	80	72	5
Red Wine Vinaigrette Dressing, 1 T	50	36	0
Robusto Italian Dressing, 1 T	70	63	0
Russian Dressing, 1 T	45	27	0
Sweet 'N Spicy French Dressing, 1 T	70	54	0
Thousand Island Dressing, 1 T	60	45	5
Wondra® Flour, 1 C	400	9	0
Yoplait® Amaretto Almond Yo Creme, 5 oz	240	90	30
Apple Custard Style Yogurt, 6 oz	190	36	15
Apple-Cinnamon Low-fat Breakfast Yogurt, 6 oz	220	36	10
Banana Yogurt, 6 oz	190	36	20
Bavarian Chocolate Yo Creme, 5 oz	270	99	30
Berries Low-fat Breakfast Yogurt, 6 oz	230	36	10
Blueberry Custard Style Yogurt, 6 oz	190	36	15
Blueberry Yogurt, 6 oz	190	36	20
Boysenberry Custard Style Yogurt, 6 oz	190	36	15

	CAL	FAT (Cal)	CHOL (mg)
Cherries Jubilee Yo Creme, 5 oz	220	72	30
Cherry Custard Style Yogurt, 6 oz	190	36	15
Cherry w/Almonds Low-fat Breakfast Yogurt, 6 oz	210	27	10
Lemon Custard Style Yogurt, 6 oz	190	36	15
Lemon Yogurt, 6 oz	190	36	20
Mixed Berry Custard Style Yogurt, 6 oz	190	36	15
150 Blueberry, 6 oz	150	<9	5
150 Cherry, 6 oz	150	<9	5
150 Peach, 6 oz	150	<9	5
150 Raspberry, 6 oz	150	<9	5
150 Strawberry, 6 oz	150	<9	5
150 Strawberry-Banana, 6 oz	150	<9	5
Orange Custard Style Yogurt, 6 oz	190	36	15
Peach Custard Style Yogurt, 6 oz	190	36	15
Pina Colada Custard Style Yogurt, 6 oz	190	36	15
Pineapple Custard Style Yogurt, 6 oz	190	36	15
Plain Yogurt, 6 oz	130	45	10
Raspberry Custard Style Yogurt, 6 oz	190	36	15
Raspberry Yogurt, 6 oz	190	36	20
Raspberries and Cream Yo Creme, 5 oz	230	81	30
Strawberry Custard Style Yogurt, 6 oz	190	36	15
Strawberry Yogurt, 6 oz	190	36	20
Strawberry-Banana Custard Style Yogurt, 6 oz	190	36	15

	CAL	FAT (Cal)	CHOL (mg)
Strawberry-Banana Lowfat Breakfast Yogurt, 6 oz	240	36	10
Strawberry w/Almonds Lowfat Breakfast Yogurt, 6 oz	210	27	10
Strawberries Romanoff Yo Creme, 5 oz	220	72	30
Tropical Fruit Low-fat Breakfast Yogurt, 6 oz	230	36	10
Vanilla Custard Style Yogurt, 6 oz	180	36	15
Zap® Pizza Cheese French Bread	308	90	3
Pizza Deluxe French Bread	323	117	3
Pizza Pepperoni French Bread	347	144	3

RESTAURANT FOODS

	CAL	FAT (Cal)	CHOL (mg)
Arby's®			
Apple Turnover	303	165	0
Bac'n Cheddar Deluxe	526	329	83
Beef 'N Cheddar	455	241	63
Cherry Turnover	280	160	0
Chicken Breast Sandwich	509	262	83
Chocolate Shake	451	104	36
Fish Fillet Sandwich	580	287	70
French Fries	215	87	8
Giant Roast Beef	531	208	65
Hot Ham 'N Cheese	292	123	45
Jamocha Shake	368	95	35

	CAL	FAT (Cal)	CHOL (mg)
Junior Roast Beef	218	77	20
King Roast Beef	467	173	49
Philly Beef 'N Swiss	460	256	107
Potato Cakes	201	116	13
Regular Roast Beef	353	133	39
Super Roast Beef	501	199	40
Turkey Deluxe	375	149	39
Vanilla Shake	330	104	32

Big Boy®

	CAL	FAT (Cal)	CHOL (mg)
Baked Potato	163	2	0
Bananas	50	1	0
Buttermilk Dressing, 1 oz	56	45	8
Broiled Breast of Chicken			
w/Lemon	225	72	68
w/salad & roll	344	78	70
Cabbage Soup, cup	37	4	3
bowl	49	5	4
Cajun Chicken	222	72	68
w/salad & roll	341	78	70
Cajun Cod, baked or broiled	304	81	89
w/salad & roll	423	87	91
Cod, baked or broiled	304	81	89
w/salad & roll	423	87	91
Chicken 'N' Vegetable Stir			
Fry	344	99	69
w/salad & roll	463	105	71
Diet Coke®	0	0	0
Dinner Salad	19	5	0
Famous Fresh Brewed			
Decaffeinated Coffee	2	tr	0
Fresh Fruit Plate	251	9	0
Grapefruit Juice, 4 oz	51	1	0
Herbal Tea	0	0	0
Mushroom Egg-Beater			
Omelette	114	45	0
Orange Juice, 4 oz	60	2	0

	CAL	FAT (Cal)	CHOL (mg)
Plain Egg-Beater Omelette	95	36	0
w/American cheese	147	72	13
Preserves	58	2	0
Rice	139	2	0
Roll	100	9	2
Scrambled Egg-Beaters	95	36	0
Skim Milk, 10 oz	110	3	6
Strawberries	63	9	0
Strawberry Vitari Shake	265	4	3
Toasted English Muffin			
w/Preserves	140	18	6
Toasted Rye w/Preserves	150	9	3
Toasted White w/Preserves	164	18	4
Toasted Whole Wheat			
w/Preserves	161	18	4
Turkey Pita	245	72	73
Vegetable Pita	164	54	8
Vegetable Stir Fry	185	54	1
Vegetarian Egg-Beater			
Omelette	116	36	0
Vitari	60	0	0

Burger King®

	CAL	FAT (Cal)	CHOL (mg)
Apple Pie	305	108	4
Bacon Double Cheeseburger	510	279	104
Breakfast Croissan'wich	304	171	243
w/Bacon	355	216	249
w/Ham	335	180	262
w/Sausage	538	369	293
Cheeseburger	317	135	48
Chicken Sandwich	688	360	82
Chicken Sandwich, no			
mayonnaise	494	180	66
Chicken Tenders, 6 pieces	204	90	47
Chocolate Shake	320	108	NK
syrup added	374	99	NK
Coffee, regular	2	0	0

	CAL	FAT (Cal)	CHOL (mg)
Diet Pepsi®	1	0	0
French Fries, regular	227	117	14
French Toast Sticks	499	261	74
Great Danish	500	324	6
Ham & Cheese Sandwich	471	216	70
Ham & Cheese Sandwich, no mayonnaise	374	117	62
Hamburger	275	108	37
Milk, 2% low-fat	121	45	18
whole	157	91	35
Onion Rings	274	144	0
Orange Juice	82	0	0
Pepsi Cola®	159	0	0
Salad, typical	28	0	0
w/Blue Cheese Dressing	184	144	22
w/House Dressing	158	117	11
w/Reduced Calorie Italian Dressing	42	9	0
w/Thousand Island Dressing	145	108	17
Scrambled Egg Platter	468	270	370
w/Bacon	536	324	378
w/Sausage	702	468	420
Scrambled Egg Platter, no Hash Browns	306	171	368
w/Bacon	374	225	376
w/Sausage	540	369	418
7 Up®	144	0	0
Vanilla Shake	321	90	NK
Syrup added	334	90	NK
Whaler Fish Sandwich	488	243	77
Whaler Fish Sandwich, no tartar sauce	354	117	57
Whopper Jr. Sandwich	322	153	41
Whopper Jr. Sandwich, no mayonnaise	274	108	37
Whopper Jr. w/Cheese	364	180	52

	CAL	FAT (Cal)	CHOL (mg)
Whopper Jr w/Cheese, no mayonnaise	316	135	48
Whopper Sandwich	628	324	90
Whopper Sandwich, no mayonnaise	482	189	78
Whopper w/Cheese	711	387	113
Whopper w/Cheese, no mayonnaise	565	252	101

Dairy Queen®

	CAL	FAT (Cal)	CHOL (mg)
Banana Split	540	99	30
"Buster Bar"	460	261	10
"Chipper" Sandwich	318	63	13
Cone, large	340	90	25
regular	240	63	15
small	140	36	10
"Dilly" Bar	210	117	10
Dipped Cone, large	510	216	30
regular	340	144	20
small	190	81	10
Double Delight	490	180	25
"DQ" Sandwich	140	36	5
Float	410	63	20
Freeze	500	108	30
"Fudge Nut Bar"	406	225	10
"Heath" "Blizzard"	800	216	65
Hot Fudge "Brownie Delight"	600	225	20
Malt, large	889	189	60
regular	760	162	50
small	520	117	35
"Mr. Misty," large	340	0	0
regular	250	0	0
small	190	0	0
"Mr. Misty" Float	390	63	20
"Mr. Misty" Freeze	500	108	30
"Mr. Misty Kiss"	70	0	0

	CAL	FAT (Cal)	CHOL (mg)
Parfait	430	72	30
"Peanut Buster" Parfait	740	306	30
"Queen's Choice" Chocolate Cone	326	144	52
"Queen's Choice" Vanilla Cone	322	144	52
Shake, large	831	198	60
regular	710	171	50
small	490	117	35
Strawberry Shortcake	540	99	25
Sundae, large	440	90	30
regular	310	72	20
small	190	36	10
Dairy Queen®/Brazier®			
BBQ Nugget Sauces	41	NK	0
Chicken Breast Fillet	608	306	78
w/Cheese	661	342	87
Chicken Nuggets	276	162	39
Double Hamburger	530	252	85
w/Cheese	650	333	95
"DQ" Hounder	480	324	80
w/Cheese	533	360	89
w/Chili	575	369	89
Fish Fillet	430	162	40
w/Cheese	483	198	49
French Fries, regular	200	90	10
French Fries, Large	320	144	15
Hot Dog	280	144	45
Hot Dog w/Cheese	330	189	55
Hot Dog w/Chili	320	180	55
Lettuce	2	0	0
Onion Rings	280	144	15
Single Hamburger	360	144	45
w/Cheese	410	180	50
Super Hot Dog	520	243	80
Super Hot Dog w/Cheese	580	306	100

	CAL	FAT (Cal)	CHOL (mg)
Super Hot Dog w/Chili	570	288	100
Tomato	4	0	0
Triple Hamburger	710	405	135
w/Cheese	820	450	145

Dunkin' Donuts®

	CAL	FAT (Cal)	CHOL (mg)
Almond Croissant	435	274	2
Apple Donut Filled w/ Cinnamon Sugar	219	107	1
Apple Spice Muffin	327	99	26
Banana Nut Muffin	327	104	23
Bavarian Creme Filled Donut	226	128	2
Bavarian Donut Filled w/Chocolate Frosting	231	85	1
Biscuit	332	206	.1
Blueberry Filled Donut	196	87	1
Blueberry Muffin	263	87	21
Bran Muffin	353	117	12
Brownie	280	118	20
Cake Munchkins w/ Powdered Sugar	69	37	.6
Cherry Muffin	317	89	31
Chocolate Cake Ring w/ Glaze	324	189	2
Chocolate Chip Cookie	129	62	6
Chocolate Croissant	502	334	1
Chocolate Frosted Yeast Ring	246	122	1
Chocolate Munchkins w/ Glaze	88	52	1
Coconut Coated Cake Ring	417	251	2
Corn Muffin	347	113	25
French Cruller w/Glaze	201	125	16
Honey Dipped Coffee Roll	348	155	1
Honey Dipped Cruller	370	208	2
Honey Dipped Yeast Ring	208	103	2
Jelly Filled Donut	274	198	2
Lemon Filled Donut	221	103	1

	CAL	FAT (Cal)	CHOL (mg)
Macaroon	351	170	3
Plain Cake Ring	319	196	2
Plain Croissant	291	199	2
Sugared Jelly Stick	332	158	2
Yeast Munchkins w/Glaze	43	16	.2

Godfather's Pizza™

	CAL	FAT (Cal)	CHOL (mg)
Original Cheese Pizza, Hot			
Slice	370	99	25
large slice	297	81	20
medium slice	270	72	15
mini slice	190	36	8
small slice	240	63	15
Original Combo Pizza, Hot			
Slice	550	216	45
large slice	437	171	36
medium slice	400	153	35
mini slice	240	63	10
small slice	360	135	30
Stuffed Pie Cheese Pizza,			
large slice	381	144	32
medium slice	350	117	25
small slice	310	99	25
Stuffed Pie Combo Pizza,			
large slice	521	234	48
medium slice	480	207	43
small slice	430	180	40
Thin Crust Cheese Pizza,			
large slice	228	63	16
medium slice	210	63	14
small slice	180	54	10
Thin Crust Combo Pizza,			
large slice	336	144	27
medium slice	310	126	25
small slice	270	117	25

	CAL	FAT (Cal)	CHOL (mg)
Hardee's®			
Apple Turnover	277	119	0
Bacon & Egg Biscuit	410	230	338
Bacon Cheeseburger	556	295	60
Big Cookie® Treat	278	138	9
Big Country Breakfast™			
Bacon	761	451	350
Ham	665	343	369
Sausage	849	630	442
Big Deluxe™ Burger	503	260	54
Big Roast Beef™	440	194	86
Biscuit 'N' Gravy™	401	197	21
Canadian Sunrise™ Biscuit	482	267	249
Cheeseburger	327	134	31
Chef Salad	309	117	172
Chicken Fillet	413	140	41
Chicken Stix™, 6 piece	234	87	35
Cinnamon 'N' Raisin™			
Biscuit	276	146	0
Cool Twist™ Cone,			
chocolate	162	42	18
vanilla	164	41	18
Country Ham Biscuit	323	160	12
Egg (only)	79	57	143
Fisherman's Fillet™	510	226	40
French Fries, large	371	171	0
French Fries, regular	197	87	0
Garden Salad	246	96	21
Ham Biscuit	300	130	17
Hamburger	244	83	20
Hash Rounds™ Potatoes	232	123	5
Hot Dog	285	128	40
Hot Ham 'N' Cheese	316	86	57
Mushroom 'N' Swiss™			
Burger	509	208	86
¼ lb. Cheeseburger	511	254	77

	CAL	FAT (Cal)	CHOL (mg)
Regular Roast Beef	312	112	68
Rise 'N' Shine™ Biscuit	257	112	0
Seafood Salad	168	21	210
Side Salad	90	4	0
Turkey Club™	426	201	45
Sausage & Egg Biscuit	503	311	179
Sausage Biscuit	426	255	25
Shake, chocolate	390	94	42
Steak Biscuit	508	263	22

Jack in the Box®

	CAL	FAT (Cal)	CHOL (mg)
Bacon Cheeseburger	705	351	85
BBQ Sauce	44	<9	0
Beef Fajita Pita	333	126	45
Blue Cheese Dressing	131	99	9
Breakfast Jack®	307	117	203
Buttermilk House Dressing	181	162	10
Canadian Crescent	452	279	226
Cheeseburger	315	126	41
Cheesecake	309	158	63
Chef Salad	325	162	142
Chicken Fajita Pita	292	72	34
Chicken Strips, 4 pieces	349	126	68
6 pieces	523	180	103
Chicken Supreme	575	324	62
Chocolate Milk Shake	330	63	25
Club Pita, excluding sauce	277	72	43
Coca-Cola® classic	144	0	0
Coffee	2	0	0
Diet Coke®	1	0	0
Double Cheeseburger	467	243	72
Dr. Pepper®	144	0	0
Egg Rolls, 3 rolls	405	171	30
5 rolls	675	388	50
Fish Supreme	554	298	66
French Fries, jumbo	442	216	16
large	353	171	13

	CAL	FAT (Cal)	CHOL (mg)
regular	221	108	8
Grape Jelly	38	0	0
Guacamole	55	45	0
Hash Browns	116	63	3
Hamburger	267	99	26
Hot Apple Turnover	410	216	15
Hot Club Supreme	524	252	82
Iced Tea	3	0	0
Jumbo Jack®	584	306	73
w/Cheese	677	360	102
Lowfat Milk	122	45	18
Mayo-Mustard Sauce	124	117	10
Mayo-Onion Sauce	143	135	20
Mexican Chicken Salad	443	189	104
Onion Rings	382	207	27
Orange Juice	80	0	0
Pancake Platter	612	198	99
Pancake Syrup	121	0	0
Ramblin'® Root Beer	176	0	0
Reduced Calorie French Dressing	80	36	0
Salsa	8	<9	0
Sausage Crescent	584	387	187
Scrambled Egg Platter	662	360	354
Seafood Cocktail Sauce	32	<9	0
Shrimp, 10 pieces	270	144	84
15 pieces	404	216	126
Side Salad	51	27	<1
Sprite®	144	0	0
Strawberry Milk Shake	320	63	25
Super Taco	288	153	37
Supreme Crescent	547	360	178
Sweet & Sour Sauce	40	<9	<1
Swiss & Bacon Burger	678	423	92
Taco	191	99	21
Taco Salad	641	342	91
Thousand Island Dressing	156	135	11

	CAL	FAT (Cal)	CHOL (mg)
Ultimate Cheeseburger	942	621	127
Vanilla Milk Shake	320	54	25

McDonald's®

	CAL	FAT (Cal)	CHOL (mg)
Apple Danish	389	161	26
Apple Pie	253	126	7
Big Mac	360	4	<.3
Biscuit w/Bacon, Egg & Cheese	483	284	263
Biscuit w/Biscuit Spread	330	164	9
Biscuit w/Sausage	467	278	48
and Egg	585	359	285
Cheeseburger	318	144	41
Chicken McNuggets	323	182	63
Chocolate Milk Shake	383	81	30
Chocolaty Chip Cookies	342	147	18
Cinnamon Raisin Danish	445	189	35
Coca-Cola® Classic	144	0	0
Cones	189	47	24
Diet Coke®	1	0	0
Egg McMuffin	340	142	259
English Muffin w/butter	186	48	15
Filet-O-Fish	435	231	47
French Fries	220	104	9
Grapefruit Juice	80	0	0
Hamburger	263	102	29
Hashbrown Potatoes	144	80	4
Honey	50	tr	tr
Hot Caramel Sundae	361	90	31
Hot Fudge Sundae	357	97	27
Hot Mustard Sauce	63	19	3
Hotcakes w/Butter Syrup	500	93	47
Iced Cheese Danish	395	196	48
McD.L.T.	680	396	101
McDonaldland Cookies	308	97	10
Milk, 2%, per 8 fl oz	121	42	18
Orange Drink	163	0	0

	CAL	FAT (Cal)	CHOL (mg)
Orange Juice	80	0	0
Pork Sausage	210	167	39
Quarter Pounder	427	212	81
w/Cheese	525	284	107
Raspberry Danish	414	143	27
Sausage McMuffin	427	237	59
w/Egg	517	296	287
Scrambled Eggs	180	117	514
Skim Milk, per 8 fl oz	90	5	5
Soft Serves	189	47	24
Sprite®	144	0	0
Strawberry Milk Shake	362	78	32
Strawberry Sundae	320	78	25
Sweet & Sour Sauce	64	3	tr
Vanilla Milk Shake	352	76	31

Red Lobster® lunch portions

	CAL	FAT (Cal)	CHOL (mg)
Atlantic Cod	100	9	70
Atlantic Ocean Perch	130	36	75
Blacktip Shark	150	9	60
Calamari, breaded & fried	360	189	140
Calico Scallops	180	18	115
Catfish	170	90	85
Cherrystone Clams	130	18	80
Chicken Breast, 4 oz	120	27	65
Deep Sea Scallops	130	18	50
Flounder	100	9	70
Grouper	110	9	65
King Crab Legs	170	18	100
Haddock	110	9	85
Halibut	110	9	60
Hamburger, ⅓ lb	320	207	105
Lemon Sole	120	9	65
Langostino	120	9	210
Mackerel	190	108	100
Maine Lobster, 1¼ lb	240	72	310
Mako Shark	140	9	100

	CAL	FAT (Cal)	CHOL (mg)
Monkfish	110	9	80
Mussels	70	18	50
Norwegian Salmon	230	108	80
Oysters, 6 raw	110	36	60
Pollock	120	9	90
Porterhouse Steak, 18 oz	1420	1179	290
Rainbow Trout	170	81	90
Red Rockfish	90	9	85
Red Snapper	110	9	70
Rock Lobster, 1 tail	230	27	200
Shrimp, 8–12 pieces	120	18	230
Sirloin Steak, 7 oz	570	432	140
Snow Crab Legs	150	18	130
Sockeye Salmon	160	36	50
Strip Steak, 7 oz	690	576	140
Swordfish	100	36	100
Tilefish	100	18	80
Yellowfin Tuna	180	54	70

Roy Rogers®

	CAL	FAT (Cal)	CHOL (mg)
Apple Danish	249	104	11
Bacon & Tomato Dressing, 1 T	136	108	NK
Bacon Cheeseburger	581	353	103
Biscuit	231	109	<5
Black Coffee	0	0	0
Blue Cheese Dressing, 1 T	150	144	NK
Breakfast Crescent Sandwich	401	246	148
w/bacon	431	267	156
w/ham	449	265	165
w/sausage	557	375	189
Brownie	264	103	10
Caramel Sundae	293	77	23
Cheese Danish	254	110	11
Cheeseburger	563	336	95
Cherry Danish	271	130	11
Chicken Breast	412	213	118

	CAL	FAT (Cal)	CHOL (mg)
Breast & Wing	604	328	165
Drumstick/Leg	140	72	40
Thigh	296	176	85
Thigh & Leg	436	248	125
Wing	192	115	47
Chocolate Shake	358	92	37
Coke®, 12 fl oz	145	0	0
Cole Slaw	110	62	<5
Crescent Roll	287	159	<5
Diet Coke®, 12 fl oz	1	0	0
Egg & Biscuit Platter	394	239	284
w/bacon	435	266	294
w/ham	442	257	304
w/sausage	550	368	325
French Fries, regular	85	122	42
large	357	166	56
Hamburger	456	255	73
Hot Chocolate, 6 fl oz	123	18	35
Hot Fudge Sundae	293	77	23
Hot Topped Potato, plain	211	2	0
w/bacon 'n cheese	397	195	34
w/broccoli 'n cheese	376	163	<19
w/oleo	274	66	0
w/sour cream 'n chives	408	188	310
w/taco beef 'n cheese	463	196	37
Iced Tea	0	0	0
Large Roast Beef	360	107	73
w/Cheese	467	188	95
Lo-cal Italian, 1 T	70	54	0
Macaroni	186	96	<5
Milk, 8 fl oz	150	74	33
Orange Juice, 7 fl oz	99	2	0
10 fl oz	136	3	0
Pancake Platter, w/syrup & butter	452	137	53
w/bacon	493	165	63
w/ham	506	156	73

	CAL	FAT (Cal)	CHOL (mg)
w/sausage	608	266	94
Potato Salad	107	55	<5
Ranch Dressing, 1 T	155	126	NK
Roast Beef Sandwich	317	92	55
w/Cheese	424	173	77
RR Bar Burger	611	355	115
Salad Bar			
Bacon Bits, 1 T	24	9	33
Broccoli, ½ C	20	0	0
Cheddar Cheese, ¼ C	112	81	30
Chinese Noodles, ¼ C	55	25	NK
Croutons, 2 T	70	0	0
Cucumbers, 5–6 slices	36	0	0
Chopped Eggs, 2 T	55	36	180
Green Peas, ¼ C	7	0	0
Green Peppers, 2 T	4	0	0
Lettuce, 1 C	10	0	0
Macaroni Salad, 2 T	60	32	<4
Mushrooms, ¼ C	5	0	0
Potato Salad, 2 T	50	27	<3
Shredded Carrots, ¼ C	42	0	0
Sliced Beets, ¼ C	16	0	0
Sunflower Seeds, 2 T	157	119	0
Tomatoes, 3 slices	20	0	0
Strawberry Shake	315	92	37
Strawberry Shortcake	447	173	28
Strawberry Sundae	216	64	23
1000 Island Dressing, 2 T	160	144	NK
Taco Bell®			
Bean Burrito	360	98	14
Green	354	98	14
Beef Burrito	402	156	59
Green	396	156	59
Beef Tostada	322	176	40
Green	316	176	40

	CAL	FAT (Cal)	CHOL (mg)
Bellbeefer	312	118	39
Green	307	118	39
Burrito Supreme	422	169	35
Green	416	169	35
Burrito Supreme Platter	774	333	79
Green	762	333	79
Cheesarito	312	115	29
Combo Burrito	381	127	36
Green	375	127	36
Double Beef Burrito			
Supreme	464	205	59
Green	459	209	59
Enchirito	381	181	56
Green	370	181	56
Fajita Steak Taco	235	98	14
w/Guacamole	269	119	14
w/sour cream	281	138	14
Hot Taco Sauce, canned	2	.3	0
packet	3	1	0
Jalapeno Peppers	20	2	0
Mexican Pizza	714	431	81
Nachos	356	173	9
Nachos Bellgrande	719	376	43
Pintos & Cheese	194	85	19
Green	189	85	19
Ranch Dressing	236	224	35
Salsa	18	1	0
Seafood Salad w/o Dressing	648	373	82
w/o Dressing/Shell	217	103	81
Soft Taco	228	106	32
Taco	184	99	32
Taco Bellgrande	351	195	55
Taco Bellgrande Platter	1002	457	80
Green	990	457	80
Taco Light	411	261	57
Taco Light Platter	1062	523	82
Green	1051	523	82

	CAL	FAT (Cal)	CHOL (mg)
Taco Salad w/o Beans	822	515	80
w/o Salsa	931	558	85
w/o Shell	525	289	82
w/Ranch Dressing	844	597	117
w/Salsa	949	559	85
Taco Sauce, canned	2	.6	0
packet	2	1	0
Tostada	243	99	18
Green	237	99	18

Wendy's®

	CAL	FAT (Cal)	CHOL (mg)
Apple Danish	360	126	NK
Apple Topping, 1 packet	130	<9	0
American Cheese Slice	60	54	15
Bacon, 1 slice	30	18	5
Bacon Cheeseburger	455	225	98
Black Pepper	0	0	0
Blue Cheese Dressing, 1 T	60	60	10
Blueberry Topping, 1 packet	60	<9	0
Big Classic	470	225	80
Big Double Classic	680	351	155
Breakfast Potatoes	360	198	20
Breakfast Sandwich	370	171	200
Buttermilk Biscuit	320	153	tr
Celery Seed Dressing, 1 T	70	54	5
Cheese Danish	430	189	NK
Cheese Sauce, 2 oz	140	108	20
Chicken Breast Fillet	200	90	60
Chicken Club	339	225	78
Chicken Fried Steak	580	369	95
Chili	240	72	25
Chives	8	0	0
Chocolate Chip Cookie	320	153	45
Cinnamon Raisin Danish	410	162	NK
Coca-Cola®	100	0	0
large	200	0	0

	CAL	FAT (Cal)	CHOL (mg)
medium	150	0	0
Coffee, 6 fl oz	2	0	0
Creamer, non-dairy, ⅜ fl oz	14	9	0
Crispy Chicken Nuggets			
cooked in animal/vegetable			
oil	290	189	55
cooked in vegetable oil	310	189	50
Decaffeinated Coffee, 6 fl oz	2	0	0
Diet Coke®	0	0	0
Diet Pepsi®	0	0	0
Double	560	270	150
w/Cheese	620	324	165
Dr. Pepper®	100	0	0
large	200	0	0
medium	150	0	0
Egg, fried, 1	90	54	230
scrambled, 2	190	108	450
Fish Fillet	210	99	45
French Fries			
cooked in animal/vegetable			
oil	310	135	15
cooked in vegetable oil	300	135	5
French Style Dressing, 1 T	70	45	0
French Toast	400	171	115
Frosty Dairy Dessert	400	126	50
Golden Italian Dressing, 1 T	50	36	0
Grape Jelly, 1 packet	40	0	0
Half & Half, ⅜ fl oz	14	9	0
Hot Chili Seasoning, 1			
packet	7	0	0
Hot Chocolate, 6 fl oz	110	9	tr
Hot Stuffed Baked Potato			
(plain)	250	18	0
Bacon & Cheese Potato	570	270	22
Broccoli & Cheese Potato	500	225	22
Cheese Potato	590	306	22

	CAL	FAT (Cal)	CHOL (mg)
Chili & Cheese Potato	510	180	22
Sour Cream & Chives Potato	460	126	15
Kaiser Bun	180	18	5
Ketchup, 1 t	6	tr	0
1 packet	12	<9	0
Kids' Meal Hamburger	200	81	35
Lemon-Lime Slice®	100	0	0
large	200	0	0
medium	150	0	0
Lemonade, 12 fl oz	160	0	0
Lettuce, 1 leaf	2	0	0
Mandarin Orange Slice®	110	0	0
large	220	0	0
medium	165	0	0
Margarine, liquid, ½ oz	100	100	0
whipped, 1 T	70	70	0
Mayonnaise	90	90	10
Milk, chocolate, 8 fl oz	190	72	225
2% lowfat, 8 fl oz	110	36	20
whole, 8 fl oz	140	72	30
Mountain Dew®	110	0	0
large	220	0	0
medium	165	0	0
Multi-Grain Bun	140	27	tr
Mustard	4	0	0
Oil, for salad, 1 T	120	120	0
Omelet #1	290	189	355
#2	250	153	450
#3	280	171	525
#4	210	135	460
¼-lb Single Hamburger Patty	210	126	75
Onion	2	0	0
Orange Juice, 6 fl oz	80	0	0
Pepsi-Cola®	110	0	0
large	220	0	0
medium	165	0	0

	CAL	FAT (Cal)	CHOL (mg)
Pickles, dill, 4 slices	0	0	0
Ranch Dressing, 1 T	50	50	5
Reduced Calorie Bacon/			
Tomato Dressing, 1 T	45	36	tr
Creamy Cucumber			
Dressing, 1 T	50	45	tr
Italian, 1 T	25	18	0
Thousand Island Dressing,			
1 T	45	36	5
Salad Bar			
Alfalfa Sprouts, 1 oz	72	0	0
American Cheese,			
imitation, 1 oz	90	63	5
Bacon Bits, 1/8 oz	10	<9	tr
Blueberries, 1 T	6	0	0
Breadsticks, 2	35	9	0
Broccoli, 1/2 C	12	0	0
Cantaloupe	18	0	0
Carrots, 1/4 C	10	0	0
Cauliflower	12	0	0
Celery, 1 T	0	0	0
Cheddar Cheese,			
imitation, 1 oz	80	54	tr
Cherry Peppers, 1 T	6	0	0
Chow Mein Noodles,			
1/2 oz	70	36	NK
Cole Slaw, 1/4 C	80	45	40
Cottage Cheese, 1/2 C	110	36	20
Croutons, 1/2 oz	60	27	NK
Cucumbers, 4 slices	2	0	0
Eggs, 1 T	30	18	90
Grapefruit, 2 oz	10	0	0
Grapes, 1/4 C	30	0	0
Green Peas, 1 oz	25	1	0
Green Peppers, 1/4 C	8	0	0
Honeydew Melon, 2			
pieces	20	0	0

	CAL	FAT (Cal)	CHOL (mg)
Iceberg Lettuce, 1 C	8	0	0
Jalapeno Peppers, 1 T	9	0	0
Mozzarella Cheese, imitation, 1 oz	90	63	tr
Mushrooms, ¼ C	4	0	0
Oranges, 2 oz	25	0	0
Parmesan, grated, 1 oz	130	81	20
Pasta Salad, ¼ C	130	54	5
Peaches, 2 pieces	17	tr	0
Pepper Rings, 1 T	2	0	0
Pineapple Chunks, ½ C	70	tr	0
Provolone Cheese, imitation, 1 oz	90	63	tr
Radishes, ½ oz	2	0	0
Red Cabbage, ¼ C	4	0	0
Red Onions, 3 rings	2	0	0
Romaine Lettuce, 1 C	10	0	0
Strawberries, 2 oz	18	0	0
Sunflower Seeds & Raisins, 1 oz	140	90	0
Swiss Cheese, imitation, 1 oz	90	63	5
Tomatoes, 1 oz	6	0	0
Salt	0	0	0
Sausage Gravy, 6 oz	440	324	85
Sausage Patty	200	162	45
Sour Cream	20	18	5
Strawberry Jam, 1 packet	40	0	0
Sugar, 1 packet	35	0	0
Sweet 'n Low®	4	0	0
Syrup, 1 packet	140	9	0
Taco Salad	430	171	45
Taco Sauce, 1 packet	10	<9	0
Tartar Sauce, 1 T	80	80	NK
Tea, hot or iced	0	0	0
Thousand Island Dressing, 1 T	70	63	10

	CAL	FAT (Cal)	CHOL (mg)
Tomatoes, 1 slice	2	0	0
Wine Vinegar, for salad, 1 T	2	0	0
White Bun	140	18	tr
White Toast, w/margarine, 2 slices	250	81	20

About the Author

Penny Mintz is a free-lance writer in the health education field and has written extensively on the subjects of diet and exercise. She has a master's degree from New York University. She lives in New York City with her husband and two sons.